10.1

11.1 , 11.2 ,11.3

Brand
YOU

Kim Richmond Richmond Marketing + Communications

Third Edition

Brand
YOU

MARKETING
REAL PEOPLE, REAL CHOICES 6e

Michael R. Solomon

SAINT JOSEPH'S UNIVERSITY

Greg W. Marshall

ROLLINS COLLEGE

Elnora W. Stuart

THE UNIVERSITY OF SOUTH CAROLINA UPSTATE

Prentice Hall
Upper Saddle River, New Jersey, 07458

AVP/Executive Editor: Melissa Sabella
VP/Editorial Director: Sally Yagan
Product Development Manager: Ashley Santora
Editorial Project Manager: Melissa Pellerano
Editorial Assistant: Karin Williams
Media Project Manager: Denise Vaughn
Director of Marketing: Patrice Lumumba Jones
Marketing Manager: Anne Fahlgren
Marketing Assistant: Susan Osterlitz
Senior Managing Editor: Judy Leale

Production Project Manager: Ana Jankowski
Permissions Coordinator: Charles Morris
Senior Operations Specialist: Arnold Vila
Creative Director: John Christiana
Interior and Cover Design: Blair Brown
Senior Art Director: Blair Brown
Composition: GEX Publishing Services
Full-Service Project Management: GEX Publishing Services
Printer/Binder: Courier/Kendallville
Typeface: 11.5/16 Palatino

Credits and acknowledgments borrowed from other sources and reproduced, with permission, in this textbook appear on appropriate page within text.

Microsoft® and Windows® are registered trademarks of the Microsoft Corporation in the U.S.A. and other countries. Screen shots and icons reprinted with permission from the Microsoft Corporation. This book is not sponsored or endorsed by or affiliated with the Microsoft Corporation.

Pearson Education Ltd., London
Pearson Education Singapore, Pte. Ltd
Pearson Education, Canada, Inc.
Pearson Education–Japan
Pearson Education Australia PTY, Limited

Pearson Education North Asia Ltd., Hong Kong
Pearson Educación de Mexico, S.A. de C.V.
Pearson Education Malaysia, Pte. Ltd.
Pearson Education, Upper Saddle River, New Jersey

Prentice Hall
is an imprint of

www.pearsonhighered.com

10 9 8 7 6 5 4 3
ISBN-13: 978-0-13-605393-4
ISBN-10: 0-13-605393-9

▶Contents

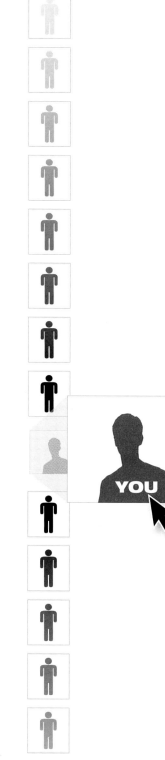

▶ Introduction

You are about to take on the mission of marketing the most important brand in the world—YOU.

Great careers don't just happen. They are carefully researched and planned, just like great brands. Even though it seems as though some brands just "happen" overnight, there was a lot of research, planning, and modification that took place before brands like YouTube, iPod, and American Eagle Outfitters became household words and brands of choice. Using these same marketing principles for your personal brand, *Brand You* will guide you through the process of how to become the brand of choice for your target employers.

You are in control of your brand and your career right now. Whether you are a freshman just beginning to think about your future, a sophomore beginning to explore different career considerations, a junior looking for an internship, a senior looking for the right first job, or an experienced executive looking to make a change, *Brand You* can help you determine the direction you want to take and how to get the job you want.

Planning your career and finding the right internship or full-time job is a process. Just like a great marketing campaign, you need a plan. You need to determine what direction you want to take, how you will position your brand, how you will advertise your brand, and how you will "close the sale" by securing the job offer you want. *Brand You*, a supplement to *Marketing: Real People, Real Choices*, by Solomon/Marshall/Stuart follows the same marketing process that unfolds in your text. You'll apply each step of the process to create and market your own unique brand.

If you want the right internship or full-time job, take charge and start building your personal brand NOW!

How to Use This Book

Planning your career and conducting a work search are part of a process. *Brand You* is designed to be an interactive workbook as well as a reference book that you can use throughout both your academic and professional careers. It employs a proven process that works for real people that you will meet throughout the book. And, the process works as well for people looking for an internship as well as for those looking for a full-time job or a career change.

To maximize your benefits from *Brand You*, read each chapter at least once. Then complete the activities in that chapter before moving on to the next chapter. To help you follow the process, the book is divided into **The 5 Steps to Real Success**.

- Step 1—Choosing Your Path
- Step 2—Researching the Market
- Step 3—Creating Your Value Proposition
- Step 4—Communicating Your Value Proposition
- Step 5—Delivering Your Value Proposition

The 5 Steps to Real Success is a step-by-step process that may take place over the course of months or years. And, chances are you will go through the process more than once...even before you graduate. For example, you may choose a career direction, send out resumés and interview for an internship, then repeat the process again when you are looking for a full-time job.

As a companion to **The 5 Steps to Real Success**, *Brand You* also includes a comprehensive Toolkit. The **Brand You Toolkit** includes valuable activities and practical examples such as a format for creating your own work plan including action plan and timeline; recommended Web sites for job searching and researching companies; do's and don'ts of on-line job searching; internship tips; sample resumés, cover letters, and thank-you notes; and FAQs—Frequently Asked Questions—about career planning and job searching. The *Brand You* Toolkit should be used frequently as it is one of the most important parts of the book.

What makes *Brand You* different is that it is more than a supplement to a textbook. Building your personal brand is a process that never ends. So use *Brand You* now, throughout your academic career, and after you graduate. You will want to revisit many of the activities at various times during your work search. You should reread many of the chapters such as those on interviewing and evaluating a job offer as you are experiencing those steps. And the information and activities in the *Brand You* Toolkit will be helpful to use again and again.

Brand You is much more than a textbook; it's the handbook for your career.

Welcome to *Brand You*!

▶ About the Authors

Kim Richmond is a senior marketing executive with over 25 years of marketing and branding experience. She was Executive Vice President, Marketing at FAO Schwarz and has held senior marketing positions at other major retailers including Zany Brainy, The Right Start, Charming Shoppes, and Sears. In addition to her extensive retail background, she also spent 7 years at Kraft Foods.

Kim is currently a principal at Richmond Marketing + Communications. Her engagements include multi-channel customer acquisition plans, catalog feasibility studies, and new product launch plans. She is also an adjunct professor in the Department of Marketing at Saint Joseph's University and a member of the Advisory Board and the Thought Leaders Panel for the Center for Consumer Research. She serves on the Scholarship Committee of the Philly Ad Club.

Kim's experience in branding, leadership, and mentorship in several industries provides real insights into how companies make hiring decisions. And her involvement in the academic arena provides valuable perspective from the student and faculty point of view.

Choosing Your Path   Step 1

This is the beginning of the development of the most important brand you will ever market—**You**. Successful brands don't just happen. Successful brands are developed as a result of research, fact-finding, insight, and thoughtful consideration. Then the brand positioning is determined and the brand message is crafted and communicated. **The 5 Steps to Real Success** outlined in *Brand You* will help you do that for your personal brand.

Do you cringe whenever someone asks you, "What do you want to do when you graduate?"

Do you give a half-hearted answer and hope you can find a job?

Do you have several areas that you want to pursue, but you don't know how to explore them?

Do you have an idea of what you want to do, but you are not exactly sure how to get a job in that field?

If you answer yes to any of these questions, *Brand You* is the perfect place to begin to answer these questions. Finding the right internship or full-time job is a process. It doesn't just happen. Getting started is the first step. And, it's never too early to start.

Step 1—Choosing Your Path includes Chapters 1–3. These chapters are filled with information, activities and resources to help you get started planning your future. Your career will most likely span decades. It's worth taking the time now to learn about what's available in the real world and which path will be best for you.

Real success starts here! ➤

1

Welcome to Brand You:
A Framework for Your Career Search

Objectives

1. What is it like in the workplace?
2. I haven't even declared my major, why should I be thinking about branding?
3. I'm not majoring in marketing. Why should I read *Brand You*?
4. How do I start to think about my future?

The Power of Brand You.

American Express, Apple, Ikea. Each of these companies has a strong brand name. Even if you haven't used the credit card, downloaded a playlist, or sat in the furniture, you probably have a clear image of each of these companies and their products and services. That's the power of branding.

Your personal brand can be as powerful as these brands. In your marketing course, you're learning about the importance of brands and how they're created. Developing a powerful brand is a process that considers the needs of customers, the value of a product, and the message that will entice customers. This supplement uses the same marketing process to create Brand You—your own personal brand. Your brand will help you to present yourself to employers as you seek internships and jobs during college, and later to differentiate yourself from all the other new college grads seeking work.

Branding is all about differentiation, about not being just a commodity. But to establish how their brand is different, marketing managers first get to know their products and their customers inside and out. *Brand You* **walks you through the steps of discovering what makes you unique.** You'll discover not only your talents, but also the benefit of those talents and the ways you can add value for your customer—your employer. When you create your own personal brand, you'll see the workplace from a different perspective, one that allows you to see more clearly the importance of how you perform and present yourself.

Many people create brands for themselves. Entertainers and athletes, for example, create personal brands. We like stars we think we know, so their branding increases the popularity (and sales) of their team or musical group. If you think about political candidates, you'll realize they brand themselves too. Many candidates seem to come out of nowhere. We know little about them or which issues they support. When candidates develop their brand, they create slogans and issue messages so we'll know something about their political views. Then they develop marketing strategies targeted toward their constituents so we'll take action and vote for them. Businesspeople create personal brands too. When we hear the names Jack Welsh (GE's power broker), Steve Jobs (Apple's founder and reviver), Bill Gates (Microsoft's founder and philanthropist), and Oprah Winfrey (entertainment's mogul who can make or break a product), their reputations enhance our image of the company brand. These unique personal brands attract employees and investors, and even help win high-level negotiations.

You may not aspire to be famous, or even a CEO, yet the same strategies can help you build your career. Creating your brand now will clarify what you can do as a student to prepare for the world of work. For example: Do you know what kind of job you want? Have you thought about the kind of company for which you want to work? Do you know what steps to take to prepare for your field? Have you even thought about your future in terms of a career as opposed to what job you want when you graduate? Reading and working through the activities in *Brand You* can help you find courses that teach needed skills, as well as other steps to increase your value to employers—like landing an internship or finding a mentor. And, of course, marketing strategies will help you succeed whenever you search for work— you'll be able to communicate your value with a clear, dynamic message.

The importance of branding doesn't stop with your first professional job. By maintaining and refining your brand over your lifetime, you will thrive no matter what the future holds. As the CEO of your own personal brand, you'll be in charge of your career, always looking for special projects and experiences that will increase your value in the marketplace.

Bill
Bieberbach's Brand

You met Bill in **Chapter 1** *of* Marketing: Real People, Real Choices. *He's vice president of corporate development for Ron Jon, which operates surfing stores in Florida, New Jersey, and California.*

▼ Q & A with Bill Bieberach

Key word:
Sincere

Distinctive competency:
Tenacity, finding "where the beef is."

My message:
"I can get the job done!"

One value I create for the company:
Results

Bill's Advice

To prepare for the workplace:
Learn to think and not react. Aristotle said, "It is the mark of an educated mind to be able to entertain a thought without accepting it."

A job-hunting strategy I would definitely use:
Determine what you enjoy and pursue a company that does that.

How a student can overcome lack of experience:
The difference between success and failure is more often a result of determination than ability. Be tenacious!

The benefit of a personal brand:
It will help wherever life may take you.

Today's Workplace

You're in Charge.
You are the CEO of your brand. It's never too early to explore your future. Your brand starts here.

Creating your own personal brand is more than a cool idea. It's a necessity in today's workplace. Welcome to today's workplace—a constantly shifting arena where there's no guarantee of employment, where jobs change faster than the click of a mouse. It's a world where new markets, new technology, and new business models will frequently alter the way you work. To adapt to new challenges, you'll need to master new subjects, quickly establish effective working relationships with a changing cast of players, and communicate with team members from different functions, often without the benefit of face-to-face interaction. This new work environment requires flexibility, continuous learning, and self-management to ensure your employability. In the workplace, you can expect

- increased pressure for innovative products and services
- a global economy and worldwide opportunities
- a networked world where work flows from one member of a virtual team to the next, sometimes spanning the globe every 24 hours
- more work options. At times, you may have a so-called full-time job, but just as likely, there will be times when you'll be an entrepreneur, indie, contract worker, free agent, or job sharer
- a participatory Web with the user as contributor (think: YouTube, Facebook, Flickr, Digg, Twitter)
- to retire later than age 65, or not at all. As we live longer, healthier lives, people will be willing to work longer, provided they can have alternative work options
- more alternative working arrangements like working from home or working from "third places"

In this changing work world, you'll need a twenty-first century mindset, one that's in tune the with current environment. You're at risk if you're expecting a permanent job that will last a lifetime. Instead, set realistic goals—strive for continuous employability. In today's workplace, you'll have to constantly re-earn your right to employment. You will need to prove and reprove continually that you have the right skills and know-how to be the "best person" for the job. Sounds like the same challenges marketers face to keep their products moving, doesn't it? The contemporary work world will require continuous marketing of your brand. You'll always be on the lookout for the next assignment, and finding ways to prepare for it.

The good news is that this is an exciting landscape, where new job titles are created every day. Just as jobs like Webmaster, chief learning officer, video game designer, and fish farmer were unheard of just a few years ago, we can't even imagine the new jobs that will appear in the next decade. Although you can't make any assumptions about job retention, you will still have security—the security that comes from being a career activist, security you create by constantly scanning the horizon for new opportunities to add value.

Whether you are self-employed or working for a firm, you are in charge of your career. The days of corporate career paths are over. It's just as well, for you can adapt to changes in the workplace much faster than a corporation can. People who count on a company to tell them what skills they need usually discover they've become obsolete when the ever-changing economy takes a new turn. Besides, you wouldn't want to put someone else in charge of your happiness, would you?

Here's a comparison of the old career mindset and the mindset you'll need as you enter the workplace. The economy may turn up or down, but we aren't likely to return to the way things were. Be ahead of your competition and get your head in the game.

Former Mindset	*Brand You* Mindset
Loyalty to a company	Loyalty to your network and profession
Job security	Lifetime employability
Career ladders	Successive projects based on skills
Learning happens at school	Learning happens everywhere, all the time
Years of experience determine your pay	Your contributions determine your pay
Boss controls your career options	You control your career options
Base work options on past experience	Base work options on emerging opportunities
Master a body of knowledge	Learn how to learn and adapt to new tasks
Stability	Mobility

How Does Branding Increase Success?

Build Your Brand On-line

The Internet provides many opportunities to build your brand. Check out the Do's and Don'ts of On-line Job Searching in the *Brand You* Toolkit.

Fundamentally, a brand is an identity that sets the product apart from the competition. We usually associate a brand with its logo (like Target's red bull's-eye) or with a slogan (like Nike's "Just do it"). In fact, some brands are so powerful that advertisers need few words to describe their products—all we see is the brand name and pictures that evoke an ideal lifestyle. Your brand can be as powerful as these. But figuring out the identity you want to communicate to your customers (potential employers) makes a lot of sense. You are a complex human being with many talents, interests, and viewpoints. Discovering which ones you want to bring to the world of work and which ones are important to employers are concrete benefits you'll achieve when you develop your own personal brand.

To develop a brand, marketers study the product to find out what the product can do. They ask, "Why would I want it?" They find the answers in the product's features. What you can do depends on your skills and knowledge. These are your "features." In building your brand, you'll want to answer the following questions: **Why would an employer want your skills? What problems can you solve?**

Next, marketers explore the benefits of the product. They ask, "What will this product do for me?" and "What can I get from this product that's better than the other products on the market?" To develop your own personal brand, think about questions like these: **What value can you add to an organization? What results will your skills achieve? What is the benefit of your solution to problems?**

When your brand is clear to you, just like a marketing expert, you'll know what to communicate to your customer. Because you will have discovered your customer's needs, you'll have confidence that your messages,

Brand:
A name, a term, or a symbol that identifies one firm's products and sets them apart from the competition.

whether delivered in a cover letter, a resumé, or an interview, will hit the mark. You'll have an effective, coherent message that will entice hiring managers to take action and hire you.

Benefits of Your Own Personal Brand

- A strong identity that you communicate to advance your career
- A focus on your customers' (that is, potential employers') needs
- An understanding of the benefits of your skills, knowledge, and experience
- The development of effective strategies to reach targeted employers
- A new attitude that puts you in charge of your career, able to adapt to change, and maintain lifetime employability

brand **YOU**
A unique identity and coherent message that sets you apart from the competition.

Applying Marketing Concepts to Brand You

Of course, developing a brand identity is only the first step. Once a brand has been created, it needs to be marketed. Here are three ways marketing concepts apply to your own personal brand:

Marketing is about meeting needs.   Jobs exist because employers need people who accomplish tasks and solve problems. Your first step in creating your own personal brand is to discover what kind of employer you want to work for and what kinds of skills and knowledge are needed to accomplish the goals of the position.

Marketing is about creating utility.   Utility creates value. The goal of your own personal brand is communicating that your skills and knowledge will be useful to employers (that is, will meet their needs). A person is hired when the value of his skills is perceived to be greater than the cost of his salary. When it comes to looking for work, you have a decision to make: do you want to be a sales machine that blankets the whole market with generic resumés, or a market-driven person who finds out who is most likely to "buy" your skills and knowledge? If you decide on the second course, your challenge is to find a target market, uncover the benefits that those employers look for in job candidates, and then develop the skills that will deliver those benefits. That's why it is important to create your own personal brand now. The more you know now about the needs of employers in your target market, the more useful you'll be when you graduate. To communicate utility, marketers develop a *value proposition*— a statement that sums up the value the customer will realize if he buys the product. *Brand You* will guide you in developing your own personal value proposition tailored to the wants and needs of the employers you're targeting.

Marketing is about exchange relationships. Work is the ultimate exchange relationship—you exchange your skills for learning opportunities and compatible work arrangements as well as financial rewards. In an exchange relationship, it's important for both the buyer (your employer) and the seller (you) to be satisfied. Job seekers sometimes make the mistake of taking the first job offered to them. But remember, you won't do your best if you don't like the work, the environment, or your boss. You'll spend at least 2,000 hours per year exchanging your skills for pay—that's a very long time if it doesn't fit your needs!

Achieving ROI

How will you measure your success as a brand? Many students' ROI (return on investment) scorecard focuses on two outcomes: their new job title and the salary they attain after graduation. (Certainly, that's not the only way to evaluate ROI—what about learning for its own sake, increased self-esteem, or the discovery of new ideas?) Like a marketing manager, you can achieve a valuable return on your investment, however you measure it, through planning. A good marketing plan is the foundation for success; it points the way to profits and return on investment. Good career planning can do the same for you. You'll avoid occupational mismatches (jobs you hate) that can lead to stress, discontent, and even depression. People who take the time to make informed career decisions are engaged in their work, committed to results, and passionate about their mission.

> *"The reason most people never reach their goals is that they don't define them, or ever seriously consider them as believable or achievable. Winners can tell you where they are going, what they plan to do along the way, and who will be sharing the adventure with them."*
>
> —*Denis Waitley*

Stepping through the Marketing Process

Creating and marketing your own personal brand is a decision process, just like any other type of marketing venture. With *Brand You*, you'll work through the steps of the process and make your own decisions about the kind of work you want—whether it's an internship or a full-time job—and the best ways to get it. Real people, people just like you, have found that this decision process actually works. Here's a thumbnail sketch of what to expect:

STEP 1 Choosing Your Path

Every great brand starts with a plan. When company executives develop strategic plans, they look at both the external environment and their internal strengths to evaluate their market position and product plans. For the career planner, the building blocks of your plan are recognizing your strengths and deciding which skills you want to use. In this step you'll get to know your product—you—and how you can apply your skills, interests, and knowledge in the workplace. You'll determine your mission, evaluate your skills, create career objectives, and identify the environment in which you work best.

STEP 2 Researching the Market

In this step, the focus is on your customer, the person who has the power to hire you. You'll discover the general characteristics employers seek in new hires. In addition, you'll examine job descriptions to uncover the specific benefits your customers are looking for. You'll look at 10 key industries and identify specific resources where you can find out more about the industry, how it functions, what kinds of jobs are available, and where you can learn more.

STEP 3 Creating Your Value Proposition

In this critical step, you'll develop a statement that summarizes the value you add to an organization. You'll learn techniques for using your value proposition during your search for work and to promote the development of your career.

Research Pays Off
You've learned how to do research papers; now you'll put your research skills to work to help identify your career path.

STEP 4 Communicating Your Value Proposition

Your value proposition becomes the basis for writing dynamic resumés and cover letters. There are samples and guidelines included to help make this easier. You'll develop an integrated marketing communication plan to get your resume to all the right people at the right time.

STEP 5 Delivering Your Value Proposition

Here's where you will learn how to prepare for and make every interview successful. And, when you get job offers, you'll have tools with which to evaluate them to make the right decision. Also, you'll understand the process of how to negotiate and accept the offer that's right for you.

Getting to Know Your Product—You

What makes you unique? This question may seem surprising, but each of us is unique. Your individuality is based on your particular constellation of characteristics—that is, your skills, interests, and personality. In the next few chapters, you'll have an opportunity to discover what makes you unique. Armed with this information, you'll be able to present yourself to employers in a compelling way. After cataloging your talents, you'll be able to describe the types of problems you can solve and the value you bring to an organization. This is an important step in creating your own personal brand.

There's another important reason to discover your talents. You may know precisely what you want to do upon graduation, but many college students have only a vague idea of their career goal, such as, "I want to go into business." But what exactly do you want to do in the business world? Do you want to manage a brand, acquire venture capital, or supervise a production team? Employers expect you to know what work you want to do, and they're likely to ask you why this career field interests you. So whether your career goal is quite definite or you're not sure at all, completing the activities in *Brand You* will increase your confidence in your goal or help you discover a goal to pursue.

We've talked about the exchange relationship between you and an employer. People find satisfaction in their work when they know what they want from the exchange. Many people want more than "just a job." They want work that feels important, that makes a difference, and even work that is meaningful or provides a sense of calling. Your work will matter to you if it is aligned with your personal values. Values describe the things you want to get from work—the assets on your side of the exchange ledger. So, the first activity, which follows on the next page, gives you an opportunity to consider what you value.

↻ exploring values

Meiko and Richard have different values, and they are reflected in their work environments.

Meiko is part of an organization that is structured around teams rather than a typical organizational hierarchy. Work is distributed to more than 100 project teams. Team members are located around the globe and meet in cyberspace to work creatively and solve problems. Team roles are defined by each person's expertise. The team operates with very few rules. The ability to get resources and results depends on Meiko's ability to persuade others to support her. Meiko enjoys the variety of projects, her role as team leader, and developing leading-edge skills.

Notes to **Myself**

2

Planning Your Career:
Setting Your Direction

Objectives

1. How do I develop a career plan?
2. What are my professional strengths?
3. How can I find career opportunities in trends?

Are you actively planning your career, or are you among the "hang out and hope" category of college students? Students in the hang-out-and-hope group avoid thinking about their future and hope that by graduation day they'll be inspired by a job title that grabs them or will miraculously have a job handed to them on a silver platter. Things rarely work out that way. **Leaving your career decisions until your senior year is risky.** Without a clear sense of direction, you'll miss important opportunities to find mentors among your professors, internships with companies that might hire you, or contacts that could lead to job offers.

As you learned from your *Marketing: Real People, Real Choices* text, "Careful planning enables a firm to speak in a clear voice in the marketplace so that customers understand what the firm is and what it has to offer. . . ." As CEO of your own personal brand, you also want to speak in a clear voice so that employers (your customers) understand who you are and what you have to offer. **Actually, this is the whole point of developing your own personal brand.**

Planning crystallizes your dreams. Your career ideas are transformed from a blur of vague possibilities to a clear vision of what you intend to accomplish. Creating a career plan is a series of decisions, starting with your personal mission statement and culminating in specific career goals. But career plans, like business plans, require action to become a reality. To achieve your goals, you'll need to drill down from the big picture of your career plan to the details—the actions you'll need to take to make your plan a reality. With each step in the process, your career choice will take shape and become clearer. As you work out the details, you'll get a good view of what it will be like to do the work. Then one of two things will happen. Either you'll be more confident about your choice, or you'll realize you need to research a different profession or industry. The latter outcome can be frustrating—but better to find it out during the planning stages than after you've accepted a job!

Businesses deliberately choose a time frame of five years for their strategic plans. In today's rapidly changing world, longer views usually prove to be meaningless. The probability of accurately forecasting developments in technology, business practices, and customer expectations beyond five years is very low. A relatively short time frame gives businesses the flexibility to adapt to changes as they occur. A five-year plan for your career is about the right length of time, too. You also need a plan that is flexible enough to adapt to changes in the workplace. Beyond five years, it's hard to predict what may happen in your job, your company, your profession, or your industry. In addition, your own personal interests and needs are likely to change over your lifetime. There will be times when your career is front and center, and times when it may take a back seat to raising a family, getting an advanced degree, or some other interest.

Although businesses look at five-year time frames for their strategic plans, they actually review and revise them every year. After all, within one year, a new start-up can grab market share or a new technology can offer new opportunities. You should review your career plan every year, too. That way you'll be able to make incremental changes to your plan. It's much easier to make minor adjustments than to discover too late that your skills are obsolete and you have to start in an entirely new career direction.

We often hear people ask, "What do I want to be when I grow up?" If they're changing careers, the question is modified slightly to "What do I want to be *this time* when I grow up?" Career planning isn't about *being* anything—you're already a real live human being. It's about *doing*. Rephrase the question to **"What do I want to do with my skills and knowledge now?"** With this question in mind, you'll be able to create a flexible plan that allows you to adapt to changes in the workplace—and there will be many! While spending 30 years in the same job may have been okay for your grandparents, it's not likely to be the way your career will unfold. And, besides, today many people think spending 30 years in the same job sounds like a life sentence.

The Right Question
Students often start their career planning by asking the question, *"What do I want to be when I grow up?"* A question that fits our changing times better is, *"What do I want to do now?"* This keeps you open to exciting possibilities that will develop.

Define Your Mission

Organizations start their strategic plans with a mission statement. The mission defines the organization's overall purpose and what it hopes to achieve in terms of its customers, products, and resources. Like an organization's mission statement, your mission statement defines your purpose. It should be narrow enough to give you a sense of focus, but broad enough to adapt to future opportunities. **A mission statement that expresses your overall purpose and what you hope to achieve will help guide your search for a career choice now and in the future.**

Your mission statement can serve as your inner career compass, guiding your decisions now and in the future. Lynn Perez-Hewitt says she belongs to the Pinball Wizard School of Career Planning. A glance at her resumé reveals seemingly disconnected work. Among other things, she's worked as a stockbroker, marketing consultant, and an executive for a nonprofit organization. But Lynn has an inner compass, a passion to **"live life fully, love fully, and share fully."** Lynn says she follows opportunities that appeal to her, as long as they fit her mission. There is also an underlying theme to her choices: through her work, she influences people in a positive way. She tackles every project with enthusiasm and shares her knowledge and creative ideas with colleagues, friends, and college students. While at first glance it looks as though Lynn bounces from one thing to another, a closer look reveals there's a mission below the surface.

Read Chris' profile containing her mission statement and the real-life profile of Sheryl. These two mission statements reflect the differences in Sheryl's and Chris's personalities. Sheryl knew she wanted to do a variety of things, yet she liked the idea of having a mission statement to express her purpose and provide continuity to her life. At this time, Chris thinks she will try a variety of marketing opportunities during her career, but thinks marketing will always be her focus. Each mission fits the person who created it.

Your top values will give you some clues about a mission that describes your purpose for working. (*Hint:* Refer to Activity 1.1.) For example, if your top value is Community, you might try a mission statement similar to this: **"To support community activities that sustain our environment."** That would give you many options, such as working for the Environmental Protection Agency (EPA), starting a community garden in a low-income neighborhood, promoting a new technology to reduce pollution, or implementing new forest management practices. As varied as these options are, each is aligned with the mission.

To Develop Your Mission, Think About:

- What's important to you
- Who you are
- What you stand for
- What you like to do
- Why you want to do it

Resources for Discovering Trends:

www.bls.gov: U.S. Bureau of Labor Statistics

www.bls.gov/oco: *The Occupational Outlook Handbook*

www.economist.com: weekly journal from England about world and national economics

www.fastcompany.com: career articles geared toward young executives

www.wfs.org: World Future Society

www.cnn.com: current events and business news

www.npr.org: National Public Radio often carries features about careers

www.rileyguide.com: comprehensive site for linking to good career sites

www.salary.com: career information including salary

Trade magazines, newspapers such as *BusinessWeek, Wall Street Journal*

Success

It's not just doing your job—it's caring about it, the people you work with, and the results you achieve. Success requires a large dose of self-discovery to find what you really care about.

ACTIVITY 2.3 Finding Opportunities in Trends

Instructions: Choose four trends that could affect the career field you're considering. Then decide what the impact of each trend might be. Finally, brainstorm career opportunities that might result. This exercise is fun to do with friends or classmates, and a group helps generate more ideas.

Trend	Impact	Opportunity
Males between the ages of 18 and 34 are watching less TV. They're spending more leisure time with TiVo and video games.	This prime marketing target is viewing fewer TV ads.	Create and sell advertising in new media; e.g., TiVo, video games, on-line game sites.

Your Career SWOT

Now that you've identified your mission and your strengths (skills), and discovered some trends that may impact your career, you're ready to try out your personal SWOT analysis.

Chris's SWOT analysis is shown below. She used her Skills Inventory and work experiences to identify her strengths. She read several Web articles about marketing to identify threats and opportunities. In spite of the threats, she's now even more excited about her career field.

Student Profile—Chris

Strengths	• Favorite skills: Creativity, Communication, and Using Information
	• Great organizational skills—able to see the big picture and then figure out how the details relate
	• Leadership ability—often asked to lead study groups, also leader in two campus organizations
	• Good negotiator—solve interpersonal conflicts in study groups and at work
	• Persuader—often get people to agree with my point of view
	• Enthusiastic, creative
	• Learning marketing theory, strategies
Weaknesses	• Sometimes impatient waiting for people to catch up to my ideas
	• Could be a better listener
	• Have so many interests, it's hard to focus on a goal
Opportunities	• Large number of people retiring, most of whom are Web-savvy
	• Web-based marketing is growing
	• New devices, like handhelds, could be a new resource for marketing
	• More businesses realizing the value of marketing
Threats	• Web-based marketing is a popular field—competition for jobs

3

Choosing the Right Work Environment:
How to Find the Right "Fit"

Where you work is just as important as what you do. When making career choices, many people think about the kind of work they want to do, but don't think about where they want to do it. The same work performed in two different companies can feel very different.

Every organization has a distinct culture that affects employees and how they do their work. In other words, one company "feels" different from another. Just as your friends have different personalities—one is easy-going, humorous, and fun seeking while another is intense, serious, and analytical—organizations have personalities too.

Objectives

1. What industry is the best fit for my style?
2. What work environment is best for me?
3. Do I want to work for a socially responsible company?
4. How can I find out if a firm is ethical?
5. How can I enter the global job market?

Organizational Culture

In *Marketing: Real People, Real Choices* you learned that values are deeply held beliefs about the right and wrong way to live. These values dictate specific rules about right and wrong and shape the behaviors of people living in a society.

Organizations also have strongly held values, including beliefs about the right and wrong way to run a business. These beliefs are strongly influenced by the values of the founders, and often survive long after the founder has placed the reins of the business in someone else's hands. Over time, these beliefs become assumptions that nearly everyone in the organization takes for granted. These beliefs and assumptions are so strongly held that is difficult to change them. In fact, many companies hire organizational consultants to flush out these assumptions (often hidden from consciousness). A company's collective assumptions must change before it is able to make major changes in the way it does business. In other words, these assumptions, if they are no longer viable, can be the downfall of any company trying to change its business plan, marketing strategy, or financial base.

You can think of an organization's culture as "the way we do things around here." You will find that many organizations have deeply ingrained ways of behaving, including everything from dress codes to managing the supply chain. For example, in bureaucratic organizations, new ideas often have to run up the appropriate chain of command and receive approval before they can be implemented. In other organizations, employees have more freedom to try out a new idea and see how it works.

Carol had worked in various marketing positions for an established toy manufacturer. She honed her skills as a market researcher/analyst for several of its product lines. She sometimes suggested new marketing strategies, but people above her resisted untested ideas. After eight years with the same employer, Carol used time during maternity leave to assess her work and reexamine her career goals. First, she wanted a shorter commute. Second, she realized she had learned just about all she could from her current employer and was ready for a change. A colleague suggested she apply for a marketing management position for a large restaurant chain. Even during her job interview, Carol noticed a difference in culture. She was introduced to people she passed in hallways, who were friendly and smiling and appeared enthusiastic. People talked about their personal lives as well as their work. Carol accepted the position and realized right away that people at the firm worked hard, but they had fun while doing it. This was very different from the serious, traditional, and analytical environment of her former employer. Early in her new job, her manager suggested she speak up more in team meetings. "You have good ideas to contribute; don't keep them to yourself." Today she is much happier in this new culture, able to implement new ideas and let her personality shine.

With practice, you'll be able to recognize cultural differences in an interview. **You'll receive two benefits from paying attention to corporate culture: (1) you'll be able to decide if this is the right place for you; and (2) you'll be able to tailor your interview responses.** If the culture seems cutting-edge, fast-paced, and innovative, you can emphasize staying current, learning new skills, and being creative. On the other hand, if the company is well-established, and the culture seems formal and everyone is well-organized, you can discuss fitting in, following guidelines, and being a team player.

Comparing Cultures

Consider these two companies and compare their different cultures. One is a global firm with 50,000 employees. It has finance, marketing, sales, and human resources departments at each location. It has the resources to invest in products that might take 20 years to develop. As a mature player in a competitive market, the emphasis is on process improvement. Employees are required to attend training classes in new technologies and even skills like team development. There are manuals everywhere, in notebooks and on the intranet, detailing every procedure. Suppliers adhere to strict specifications and even contribute to the design of new products. At all levels of the organization people work in cross-functional teams to find more efficient ways to design, produce, ship, and support products. The company invests heavily in business professionals who analyze processes, measure productivity, and develop strategies to achieve greater profitability. The workforce includes long-term careerists valued for their engineering or technical skills. Changing the culture to match today's fast-paced reality is an evolutionary process. As one team leader put it, "Making significant changes around here is like turning around a battleship—it takes time."

The second company is a three-year-old biotech firm. Started by two academic researchers, this is their first venture into the world of business. It now employs two hundred workers, most of whom are young and well educated. The emphasis is on marketing and sales. Procedures change frequently, and people make decisions on the fly. This is a fast-paced environment, often requiring long hours to meet exacting customer specifications. Many employees create their own job responsibilities because job descriptions are sketchy at best. Frustrated by the lack of structure and changing priorities, many employees don't stay long. The founders of the company are always looking for new technologies and continuously search for venture capital. They hope to buy other biotech start-ups to stave off a takeover.

Two Organizational Cultures

The culture of the organization and the temperament of the people who work there have a strong influence on the nature of the workplace. Here are some factors that influence organizational culture:

- **The location of the business** as well as the look of the building and the design of its workspaces. Does everyone have a cubicle or office, or are workspaces open and configured around a hub?
- **The occupation and personality of key players.** Does the company revere its scientists, or its dealmakers?
- **The management philosophy and style.** Do managers micromanage every detail, or do they set goals and then step aside so employees can accomplish them?
- **The history of the company.** What are the values of company heroes? Do people cite lessons learned from past successes and failures?
- **The organization's size.** Is work performed in well-defined silos or do employees have broad responsibilities because the organization is small?
- **Risk-taking.** Does the company take risks, or is it financially conservative? What are the consequences if an employee makes a mistake?

The Buzz
To find out what employees
say about their employer, go
to **www.vault.com.**

- **Ethics.** Does the company have a code of ethics? Do employees follow the code?
- **Social responsibility.** Does the organization contribute to the public good? Is it a good citizen in its community?
- **Ownership.** Is it publicly traded, or privately held?

Characteristics	Established *Fortune* 100 firm	Start-up biotech firm
Types of workers	Stability seekers	Autonomy seekers
Employment contract	Long-term employment Good benefits and pay	High turnover Lower pay, some benefits and good stock options
Education	Moderate, with extensive training opportunities	High, with little investment in employee training and development
Predictability	Established guidelines	Continuous change
Emotional tone	Calm	Sometimes frantic
Business strategy	Invest for the future	Stay on the leading edge, take risks, innovate
Accountability	Productivity is measured	Too busy building an enterprise to measure
Management style	Mentoring and coaching	You're on your own

Cracking the Code of Organization Culture

Some clues are evident in interviews, but it pays to research a company's culture beforehand. To find a great fit, think about what's important to you. Do you care about social responsibility? How important are the firm's ethics? What makes a company great in your eyes?

There are several ways to investigate a company's culture:

Company Web sites. You may be able to get a glimpse at a firm's culture by browsing its Web site. Is the site devoted entirely to products and services, or does it also feature employee contributions? Does it depict a diverse workforce? Is there any mention of ethics or social responsibility? What company characteristics does it promote as it tries to recruit you?

Research. Business magazines, Lexis-Nexis, and trade journals are excellent resources. Articles may not describe the culture directly, but with a little analyzing you may be able to infer something about a company's culture. Each year *Fortune* magazine publishes the following lists: 100 Best Companies to Work For (based on benefits, salaries, training budgets, work/life balance, and stock performance), America's Most Admired Companies, Best Companies for Minorities, and Global Most Admired Companies.

Network with an insider.   One of the best resources for the inside scoop is to talk to someone who works at a company you are considering. The time to do this is before you interview—that's when people will be more candid about what it's like to work there. In later chapters, we'll discuss the power of networking.

Observe the culture when you interview.   If more than one person interviews you, this is probably a team environment. Ask for a brief tour. Notice people's dress and how their workspaces are decorated. See if you can sense the general atmosphere, noting whether people seem calm or tense. Are people working together, engaged in conversations, or working alone? After your interview, spend time imagining what it would be like to work in this environment.

Finding Your Place in 10 Industry Sectors

Another factor that influences culture is the industry of the enterprise. We'll take a look next at 10 industries, and discuss some cultural issues that generally are true for the industry. The descriptions are only general guidelines. Factors such as size, management philosophy, and style of the CEO influence a company's culture. **Remember, you're looking for a fit.** One industry isn't better than another; it's a matter of which culture matches your personality and work preferences. As you read the descriptions that follow, consider:

THESE SITES: for more info about industries:
www.bls.gov/oco
www.online.onetcenter.org
www.hoovers.com

- What words appeal to you? What turns you off?
- Think about how well the culture matches your talents, work style, and personality. Ask yourself, "Would I fit in here?"
- Examine how work functions and industries combine to form different environments. For example, compare a marketing position in a high-tech firm with one in a retail chain. Marketing departments tend to have a distinct culture, but that environment is influenced by the industry where it resides.

Agriculture, Mining, and Construction

Examples: *agribusiness, petrochemical, forestry, aquaculture, residential/commercial construction, and global military installations*

Do you enjoy seeing concrete results? Do you enjoy working outdoors and being physically active? These industries are populated with practical people who take pride in their skills and accomplishments. Once relying on time-honored techniques, new materials and methods are creating new challenges for workers. This sector consists mainly of small, family-owned businesses, but global conglomerates such as Archer Daniels Midland (ADM), Bechtel, and Halliburton offer opportunities for world travel. College grads can find work in project management, finance, marketing, and sales. In small firms, managers often wear several hats.

Manufacturing/Research and Development

Examples: *automotive, aerospace, clothing, pharmaceuticals, computers*

Whether it's process, chemical, electrical, or computer engineering, are you a math or science whiz who thrives on developing logical solutions to complex problems? If you aren't bound for engineering, do you enjoy working with analytical, logical personalities? Engineers and research scientists are often the stars in these firms, sometimes earning as much as a V.P. because of a breakthrough in technology. In these environments, all work is expected to meet strict time lines, tight budgets, and quality-control standards. The mantra in these organizations is "Do more with less." This sector is a fit for detail-oriented, level-headed problem-solvers. Employment is fairly stable, although downsizings occur with fluctuations in the economy. If you're looking for a stable environment with opportunities for advancement, this sector might fit you. Organizational cultures vary within this sector, depending on whether the firm is a small start-up or a mature operation with a large investment in machinery and equipment.

Sales/Marketing

Examples: *autos, clothing, food, retail stores, and Web-based sellers, cosmetics*

Do you enjoy knowing a product or brand inside and out? Do you have the quantitative and analytical skills necessary to measure the effectiveness of marketing campaigns? Do you want an opportunity to express your creativity? Work includes deciding how and to whom to sell products, improving the supply chain, and creating a "brand experience." For sales people and marketers, performance and profitability are the name of the game. There is intense competition in the marketplace and within the organization. The Internet plays a significant role in building brands and relationships with consumers. Firms frequently restructure, and employees must be flexible and ready to retool themselves at a moment's notice. There is little tolerance for failure. This sector is a good match for high achievers with creative ideas and high energy. If you thrive in a fast-paced, fluid environment, this may be the sector for you.

Information/Media/Entertainment

Examples: *publishing, mass media, software publishing, telecommunications, advertising, public relations, film*

Do you enjoy expressing your ideas and participating in creative activities? Do you like working with words, ideas, and images? People in the creative end of these firms prefer practicing their craft to amassing financial rewards. They identify strongly with their work and derive their status from being recognized for their creative contributions. Their ambition is to rise to more prestigious outlets or high-profile assignments, rather than management. They're interested in "the buzz" and are always up on the latest trends and technologies, especially the Internet. Although creativity and fresh ideas are important, technical skills like editing, researching, and reporting are the building blocks of these professions. Entry positions are usually in these areas—once you pay your dues, you can move on to more creative work. This sector is extremely mobile—people frequently move from one media outlet to another, and much of the work is freelance or project-based. Most people identify with their profession, not their employer.

Finance/Insurance

Examples: *banking, commercial real estate, insurance, securities, venture capitalists*

Do you have a detailed mind and a full understanding of the financial world? This sector requires personal integrity and self-confidence, because you will be entrusted with large sums of money and proprietary information. Your image is important—you must look the part. Be prepared for some long hours and perhaps sleepless nights. For agents and brokers, this is a fast-paced, demanding world, where the next deal is everything. Quieter types usually work behind the scenes as analysts, auditors, or actuaries, or in more sedate environments like insurance or retail banking.

Professional and Business Services

Examples: *computer systems design, employment services, benefits consultants, management, scientific, and technical consulting, public accounting, and legal firms, client services organizations*

Do you enjoy selling your expertise and knowledge? Can you uncover client needs and design solutions to their problems? Do you have excellent communication skills? Work environments in this sector are very professional, for reputation is critical. Success is determined by leading-edge technical skills, a talent for building client relationships, and internal self-management.

Student Profile—Chris

After her research, Chris decided she would focus her career search on two types of companies: marketing consulting firms and consumer products companies with a strong Web presence. She thinks the second option would be a good way to learn the business, but realizes that in the long term, she'll be happier in a small firm (perhaps her own) with a strong reputation.

The cultures of firms vary, usually dependent on their size and the managing partner's style. Many firms rely on large pools of knowledgeable workers to fill rank-and-file positions. They often work long hours to meet individual client needs. It can take several years to move into partner status, when you are rewarded with prestigious clients and shorter hours. Some consultants work in teams at the client's place of business for several weeks or months. Large public accounting and human resource consulting firms house many specialties under one roof, providing opportunities for lateral moves. Many young professionals move from a consulting firm to a staff position in a client organization.

Education and Health Services

Examples: *edutainment (video, e-learning), psychological and social services, educational institutions, hospitals, clinics, fitness trainers, nutritionists*

Are you looking for work that makes a difference in the lives of those you serve? People in this sector work with their hearts as well as their minds. Expertise and skills are paramount and continuous learning is required to stay current with new methods and technology. Organizations in this sector set high professional standards. Most people are not motivated primarily by money, but by a calling to improve people's lives. If you are compassionate, dedicated, and able to keep your spirits up, this sector might fit you best.

Leisure/Hospitality/Culture

Examples: *restaurants, hotels, resorts, recreational facilities, parks, entertainment museums, art galleries*

Do you like serving people or helping them enjoy their time off? Can you accommodate guests with grace, and provide great customer service? When things go wrong, you'll have to stay cool under pressure. Many jobs in this sector are low paying and routine, yet many people enjoy this work and the fact

My Career Journal

What did you learn when you studied the 10 industry sectors?

_____

_____

_____

_____

_____

_____

_____

_____

_____

_____

Reality check: Refer back to **Activity 3.1 Work Environment** and compare it to the industry sector you prefer. Is there a match between your work preferences and the industry environment? Where is there a mismatch? Can you live with the industry after all?

_____

_____

_____

_____

_____

Do you think working overseas is important for your career? If so, what resources do you plan to explore?

_____

_____

_____

_____

_____

_____

Notes to **Myself**

Researching the Market

Step 2

Whether you are looking for an internship or a full-time job, you will need to do some research to determine which industry or industries you want to pursue and which companies will be on your target list.

Are you wondering where to start your research? Chapters 4–7 include valuable information including the best Web sites for your research. You'll be surprised to learn about many interesting companies and what they have to offer. And, you'll learn how the hiring process works so you can anticipate and be prepared for each step.

Chapter 4 – Career Information and Research is especially helpful since it contains specific information about how to use both on-line and off-line resources for your job search. It includes Gathering Information On-line – 11 Tips for Finding the Right Web Sites. In addition, the *Brand You* Toolkit includes a listing of recommended Web sites with general job boards as well as industry-specific sites and professional organizations. The chapter also includes Off-line Resources You Shouldn't Skip – 6 Places to Explore in Person.

You have learned how to do a research paper for your classes, now learn how to do research for your future. The roadmap and resources are in the next 4 chapters.

Research has its rewards. ➤

4
Career Information and Research:
Know Where to Look

Objectives

1. How do I gather relevant career information?

2. What trends will affect my career?

3. How can futurist research help in career decision-making?

4. Where do I look to find out about industries and companies?

5. How can I evaluate a career choice?

6. What research should I do for an internship versus a full-time job?

So far, you've been developing your own personal brand the same way a marketing professional goes about it, by first looking inward and identifying your strengths and determining your preferences. Now it's time to look outside at the world of work. In this chapter, you'll explore one career field to decide if it meets your criteria for great work. In later chapters, you'll narrow your focus to specific employers so you understand your customers' value needs. The more you know about the needs of an employer, the more you'll be able to target your brand.

Knowledge Is Power

Too often college students can't get where they want to go (a meaningful job) because they don't know what that is or where to find it. They think they are ready to job hunt, when actually they are ready to explore careers. Recruiters can easily spot a person like this—they are unclear about how they want to apply their skills and knowledge, so of course they can't express real enthusiasm for the job at hand. Since so much career information is available at your fingertips, employers lose patience with applicants who don't know what they want. When it comes to job hunting, knowledge is definitely power.

In this chapter, we'll help you avoid being a "lost" student. What these job seekers lack is the *information* needed to make good career decisions. You can get a jump start on your career by sharpening your focus now. **Take the time to thoroughly research careers and drill down to data that will be relevant**

to your eventual search for work. When you reach the end of your college days, you'll know where you want to go and how to get there.

Researching Like a Futurist

You learned in *Marketing: Real People, Real Choices* that "some marketing researchers, known as *futurists*, specialize in predicting consumer trends to come. They try to forecast changes in lifestyles that will affect the wants and needs of customers in the coming years. Futurists try to imagine different scenarios, or possible future situations, that might occur." When you do your career research, act like a futurist. **Go beyond discovering what's already happened; find out where the profession and industry is headed.**

Until recently, there was little need to scan the future to decide on a career. When change happened slowly over a lifetime, examining the way things were done in the past was enough. Researching a career field was a simple process. You could read publications that described the skills and abilities needed or you could talk to someone working in the field. Although these are still good methods to begin researching a career, **today you must also know about the future.**

In Chapter 1, we talked about some of the ways work is changing. We discussed the relentless pressure for faster product innovation, the emergence of a global playing field, the new capabilities in a networked world, and the development of more work options. Broad changes like these will affect nearly everyone in the world of work. Other changes will be specific to a particular industry. For example, some futurists predict that by the year 2019, personal virtual realities will be taking market share away from TV, radio, films, and other media. What impact would that have on your career if you were producing content for one of the traditional media formats?

How Futurist Research Can Help

Research into future trends is essential to ensure that changes won't catch you by surprise. Although you can't predict precisely what changes the future holds, you can be sure that no matter what career you're researching, it will change and evolve. **Follow Wayne Gretsky's advice and look ahead so you're ready when the future arrives.** Futurist research can help you in the following ways:

The Gretsky Principle
"Don't skate to where the puck is; skate to where the puck will be."

- **Improve decision-making.** When you're aware of potential opportunities or challenges that the future may bring, you can make an informed decision about whether the field is a good fit for you.
- **Create career resilience.** Examining how your career will change ensures that the career you are choosing and the education you are pursuing will continue to provide you with a viable living.

- **Uncover different ideas.** Good research uncovers various viewpoints to help you in considering the impact of trends and opportunities. It's easy to find information about a new technology; it's more difficult to stretch your thinking to forecast the impact it might have in the marketplace.

Keys to the Right Information

Whether you are considering an internship or a full-time job, the foundation of your search for great work is great research. The goal is to identify a career option or, if you have a career in mind, confirm that you have an accurate picture of that career. Knowing how to research career options is a valuable skill. Undoubtedly, there will be times in the future, either because of your own development or changes in the workplace, when you'll use these skills again.

The best place to begin is with good research strategies. Four strategies will help you gather and evaluate career information:

Focus on the big picture.

Discover possibilities.

Evaluate your assumptions.

Ask the right questions.

Focus on the Big Picture

Begin your research by examining industries and professions rather than specific job titles. Industries and professions are stable—many have survived for centuries. We may use new fuels in the future or rely less on personal cars, but we'll still need a way to get from one place to another. If you're interested in transportation, the right question may be, what alternatives are on the drawing boards?

Professions and industries exist to meet basic needs. For instance, human beings have always had a need to know what's going on in the world. We've evolved from town criers to newspaper journalists to TV reporters to blog moderators. The job titles and media have changed, but the need remains constant.

Generally, jobs change more frequently than industries or professions do. However, technology can have a big impact on a profession. Not so long ago, a staff accountant's primary responsibility was entering data into a ledger and calculating debits and credits. Today, an accountant uses a computerized system and delegates data entry to an assistant. The main function of the job now is advisory—collaborating with operations managers to find ways to reduce costs and increase profits for their area. With these changes, accountants have had to learn both technical and interpersonal skills to adapt to their new role.

As you research an industry or profession, think about the need it fulfills. Considering the changes that you read about, will the need still exist in 10 years? How will work in the industry change? In the future, will it still fit with your preferred skills? For example, some accountants are much more comfortable crunching numbers than advising business leaders. They have moved into tax accounting or other fields in which they can still rely on their computational skills.

Discover Possibilities

In Chapter 2, you completed an activity in which you identified some trends, thought about their impact, and considered opportunities that might result. Continue this kind of inquiry as you research an industry or profession. Be on the lookout for trends that will affect the field. Think about new jobs that will emerge. For example, as on-line learning becomes more widespread, what will be its impact on education? Some predict fewer teachers will be needed, and those in the classroom will act as learning guides on the side rather than as experts at the front of the room. On the other hand, think of the possibilities for people who develop educational content, graphics, and connectivity. Many predict that education will morph into edutainment.

Evaluate Your Assumptions

We all have ideas about what certain jobs are like. Your tentative career choice is based on your exposure to work, viewpoints you've heard, and things you've read or seen in the media. You may think you know a great deal about the field already (and perhaps you do), but you have probably filled in information gaps with assumptions. One goal of your research is to determine whether the facts support the opinions you've heard and the assumptions you've made.

As you conduct your research, find out what it's really like to do the work—day in and day out. To gain accurate information, it's important to recognize and put aside your assumptions. The following questions will help you:

- **What assumptions am I making about working in this field?**
- **Are my assumptions based on fact?**
- **What questions can I ask to test my assumptions?**

When our marketing student, Chris, thought about it, she realized she had assumed she would immediately be developing creative marketing ideas. When Chris decided she wanted to work in an established consumer products company, she realized she wouldn't be *the* marketing department—she'd be the junior member of a marketing team. She decided to find out the typical assignments for new hires. Chris also realized she needed to learn about the consumer products industry. She wanted to find out which products were expected to do well in the future and learn about trends that might affect people's buying habits.

Ask the Right Questions

Good research requires planning and organization. Just like a marketing professional doing research, your first task is to define the problem and specify your research objectives. What is it you want to know about the industry or profession you are researching?

As you plan your research, look for resources that will tell you things you don't already know. The resources listed in this chapter are a good starting point. A good research strategy will help you discover what a particular career field is like. You'll also want to learn what people are saying about its future.

Your research questions will be unique, depending on the field you are investigating, the amount of information you already know, and your own curiosity. Listed below are some general questions to consider asking as you do your research.

The nature of the work

- What are the types of tasks and responsibilities people have?
- What market needs does the work fulfill?
- What kinds of people tend to do well in this field?
- What are some examples of typical projects?
- What kinds of problems do people solve?

Getting started

- What type of education is generally required to enter this field?
- What college majors are suggested?
- What type of experience is helpful for entering this field?

Values

- Compensation and benefits are not the only things to consider when choosing a career. Also research the internal rewards—the reasons people say they like working in this field. Then return to Activity 1.1 in Chapter 1 to see if these rewards match your own values.
- What is the typical starting salary in this field?
- What is the salary range for people with 5 years of experience?
- Is there an opportunity to learn new skills?
- What is the work environment like?

Future opportunities

- How is technology changing this field?
- What changes are anticipated in the way work is performed?
- What factors influence advancement in this field?

Futurist Research Involves

- Focusing on the big picture
- Discovering possibilities
- Evaluating your assumptions
- Asking the right questions

Research Resources—The Best Places to Research Your Career Direction

You have learned how to do research for a paper. Now you are going to apply those skills to researching the direction you want to take for your career.

Whenever you are conducting research, use the following guiding principles:

- **Search from general to specific.** That means that first you should research industries such as the ones discussed in Chapter 3. After you identify one or two industries that are interesting to you, drill down and begin to research specialties (which are discussed in Chapter 5), then drill down again to research companies, and finally research jobs. It might sound like a lot of work, but if you keep your research focused, it will be easier and more informative to help you guide your decisions.

- **Gather information from multiple sources.** You will be investigating many areas and you want to be sure that you get the full picture. For example, if you are interested in advertising, you will most likely find some sources that talk about the excitement and creativity of the industry and you will also find some that discuss the high-risk nature of the industry. You should be aware of both sides so you can make your evaluation with complete information.

Gathering Information On-line—11 Tips for Finding the Right Web Sites

You know your way around the Internet, but do you know where to start to make your career direction decision? Here is a guide to help you identify which Web sites are worth researching. Use this framework to begin your research. Don't limit your research to only these Web sites. This should be a starting point for you. Search and find the Web sites that will help you in your research. Bookmark your favorite Web sites on your computer so you can go back to them. Right now, you are gathering information. You will learn in Chapter 12 how to use this information to create a communication plan.

Learn the Ins and Outs

Get the inside story on what works…and what to avoid on-line. Read the Do's and Don'ts of On-line Job Searching in the *Brand You* Toolkit.

11 Tips for Finding the Right Web Sites

Tip #	Topic	What to Look For	Some Suggested Web Sites
1	Industry Research	News, trends, and general information by industry	**www.hoovers.com** **www.bls.gov/oco** **www.online.onetcenter.org**
2	Career Planning	Articles, tips, advice on how to consider a career direction	Your campus career center and Web site. Your campus library may have subscriptions to many paid Web sites such as **www.hoovers.com**, **www.lexisnexis.com**, etc. Also review Web sites listed in the *Brand You* Toolkit including sites such as **www.career-advice.monster.com** **www.rileyguide.com** **www.salary.com**
3	Professional Trade Organizations	National, regional, and local organizations and associations in the industry or discipline in which you are interested, which include industry news, events, articles about influential people and recently promoted people. Professional organization Web sites are an excellent source for internship and full-time job listings.	Visit **www.associationjobboards.com** to find a listing of many professional organizations. Also visit the organization's home page as well as the job board. Also see Recommended Web sites in *Brand You* Toolkit for a comprehensive list of Web sites. TIP: Also do an on-line search for local professional organizations such as the local city advertising club.
4	Industry Trade Journals	E-mail, on-line, and hard-copy publications, which include news, events, and jobs. Most trade publications offer free e-mail newsletters and many offer free circulation of their magazine.	Ask a professor which are the best trade publications to read in the industry in which you are interested. Go to the campus library or public library and ask about the trade publications for your industry. Do an on-line search for trade publications in your industry.
5	Local Business Journals and Newspaper Web sites	News, key industry people, and financial performance of local businesses. Local job listings are also available.	Visit **www.bizjournals.com** to find the business journal Web site for the city nearest you. Visit your local newspaper's Web site and read the business section regularly.

Continues on the next page...

11 Tips for Finding the Right Web Sites

Tip #	Topic	What to Look For	Some Suggested Web Sites
6	Business Lists	Lists of top businesses in a variety of categories such as Top Public Accounting Firms, Top Advertising Agencies, Top Public Relations Agencies, Fastest Growing Companies, Best Companies to Work For, Top Companies to Start Your Career, Top Companies for Women, Top Companies for Minorities, Top Companies for Families, etc.	National lists are available from national business publications such as **www.businessweek.com**, **www.wsj.com**, **www.fortune.com**. Local and regional lists are usually available from the Web site of your local newspaper, **www.bizjournals.com** and local professional organizations and trade publications.
7	Business Directories	Directories with company listings, financial information, number of employees, key contact people in the industry, and/or geographic area of your preference.	Check your campus library for business directories in your industry. The library may have a subscription to some paid directories such as the Directory of Corporate Affiliations, Advertising Red Books, etc. Also check professional organization Web sites for business directories. For example, on the American Marketing Association Web site you can find as many as 8 different directories of companies the marketing industry by visiting **www.marketingpower.com/AboutAMA/ Publications/Pages/SpecializedDirectories.aspx**.
8	Company Web Sites	Use the business lists and directories to help identify your target companies. Check the company Web sites regularly for internships and full-time jobs.	Various
9	Professional Social Networks	Use Web sites that are focused on business networking where you can learn about a specific industry, talk to small business owners and create a network of people to ask questions and make contacts.	**www.linkedin.com** **www.ryze.com** **www.ecademy.com** **www.biznik.com** **www.womanowned.com** **www.ziggs.com** **www.jobster.com**
10	Job Boards	Use a mix of large, specialized, and industry-specific job boards.	See Recommended Web sites in *Brand You* Toolkit
11	Recruiting and Employment Companies	Look for companies that don't charge a fee to search for jobs or post your resumé	Search for employment agencies at **www. superpages.com**. They are listed by city. You can also narrow your search to your industry.

Off-line Resources You Shouldn't Skip—6 Places to Explore in Person

Don't limit your research to the Internet. There are excellent resources that are best used in person. Don't wait until you're a senior to get to know these people and places.

Tip #	Where to Go	Why to Go There
1	Campus Career Center	Your campus career center offers more resources than you think. Make an appointment and meet with a counselor to understand everything that is available. Many offer seminars and how-to clinics, job fairs, mock interviews, resumé and cover letter critiques, research resources, and general advice and guidance. You can find help for career planning, internships, and full-time jobs. Don't just scan the Web site, go check it out.
2	Campus or Public Library	Like the campus career center, the library is an excellent resource. Make an appointment with a librarian and learn about all the tools that are available for your research. Ask about which Web sites, databases, and business directories you can access through the library.
3	Campus Alumni Association	Make an appointment to meet with someone in the alumni association or the office that handles alumni affairs. Look up on your campus Web site which office handles this. Meet with the person and find out the best way to network with alumni that are currently working in the industry or industries you would like to pursue. Alumni are usually very receptive to helping undergraduates or new graduates find an internship or full-time job.
4	Networking	If you want to do effective networking, pick up the phone. Yes, you will probably follow-up via e-mail, but your initial contact should be personal. See Chapter 14 for a complete look at how to network.
5	Professional Organizations	Many professional organizations have collegiate chapters or affiliations with colleges and universities. Go to the department of your major and find out what professional organizations are on campus. Go to a meeting, event, seminar, conference, or other activity sponsored by the organization. It's a great way to get exposure to the industry and meet people who can give you more insight. Most professional organizations have reduced membership and/or event fees for students. And, if you become a member, it's a great addition to your resumé.
6	Informational Interviews	You can ask someone who is currently working in the industry if you can meet with him or her to get some insight into the industry. This is a perfect opportunity to learn and ask questions. Ask friends, professors, the alumni association, career center, or professional organization for a contact. People want to help you succeed. Take the opportunity to explore as much as you can. A word of caution, if someone agrees to meet with you, consider it a fact-finding visit. It's not the time to ask for a job.

Notes to **Myself**

5

Why Employers Buy:
How to Build Your Brand Based on Employers' Needs

Objectives

1. Exactly how do I create my own personal brand?
2. What organizational specialties are common?
3. Which specialty is best for me?
4. Should I focus on what I want or on "hot" careers?

An employer goes through the same decision process as any other consumer who is making a major purchase. In fact, you might say the decision to hire an employee is more critical than purchasing a home or car! For one thing, it often involves a bigger investment. Although many employees change jobs every two or three years, many people stay in a job longer than they stay in a house. How long an employee will stay is not the only concern a manager has. Managers know that one person can affect teamwork, morale, productivity, and therefore, the bottom line. It's no wonder the hiring process is complex!

In this chapter and the next, we'll examine how employers make hiring decisions. The more you know about how decisions are made, the better you can prepare for your work search. We won't try to influence you to become someone you're not; rather our intent is to help you understand your customer better. With this information in hand, you can develop a brand message that appeals to your targeted employers.

What motivates an employer to "buy" a new employee? The first thing to recognize is that employers aren't anxious to add personnel. People are expensive. They must be hired, trained, and managed—each phase of the process is costly in terms of time and money. Besides all that, employees have to be paid! On the other hand, every enterprise has goals it wants to achieve. When the number of people on hand limits its ability to achieve those goals, a firm decides to hire more people.

Once the need has been recognized, the hiring manager makes some decisions about the kind of person he wants to fill the position. He may talk to others in the department to get their view of the qualifications the person should have. He reviews the job description and thinks about the problems the person will solve, their relationship with customers, and other key responsibilities. With this information, he creates a list of skills and abilities he thinks the person should have in order to succeed in the position. He will define success as the ability to add value to her department, and ultimately, his bottom line.

It's true, the internal influences discussed in *Marketing: Real People, Real Choices*—such as perception, motivation, attitudes, and personality—are factors that influence the decision makers you'll meet during your search for work. However, this is a business decision, and most hiring managers will try to minimize the impact of these factors. They have a business need and they are looking for the person who can best meet that need. Interviewing is difficult enough without trying to "psych out" the individual you are talking to. **A much better strategy is to learn as much as you can about the industry, the company, and the needs of the person who has the power to hire you.** Then you'll be able to develop compelling ways to describe how you can add value to the organization.

Create Your Own Personal Brand

Through the work you've been doing and will continue to do in future chapters, you are creating your brand. Perhaps now is a good time to explain exactly what a personal brand is and what it does for your career. It's also helpful to preview the process of creating a brand. Once you see the process, you'll realize you're already well on your way to creating Brand You.

Branding is the process of determining who you are. You do this so that you can differentiate yourself from all the other college grads seeking work. In this process, you're discovering your strengths, your values, and your passions. **The result of all of this effort is your brand (developed to keep a consistent focus on your benefits)—the value you add to an organization.**

You're not creating your brand so much as you are constantly building and projecting it. Although, it's not about being phony. You're determining who you are, not inventing a new persona. Branding is deeper than manipulating other people's perceptions; it's a process of understanding your values.

Your Task in Developing Your Brand Is to Think like the Hiring Manager

Imagine a job opening in which you are interested. If you were the boss, what kind of person would you select to fill the position? What skills and knowledge would you want a new employee to have? What kinds of problems will this person need to solve? When you have enough information to answer these questions, you'll be able to market yourself to the employer's needs.

Steps for Creating Your Brand

Complete your self-assessment. Review your mission statement, skills inventory, and SWOT analysis. Distill all this information to decide your core competency. A core competency is a constellation of related capabilities that has sustainable value and broad applicability. Your core competency creates the value you add to an organization.

Decide on a target market. What industry sector? What function within the organization? Learn as much as you can about the employers in this niche. What are their needs? What benefit do they want from the person they hire?

Develop a brand message. Emphasize the benefit you add.

Develop strategies to achieve your goals. How will you communicate your brand message? How will you connect with your target market?

We've already touched on a few of these steps; the rest will be explained in subsequent chapters.

Build Your Brand

As a college student, you have many demands on your time. However, finding short periods to read the latest news in the field you've chosen will pay off. It will open your eyes to a variety of possibilities and alert you to actions you can take while you're in school to further your career. Remember, employers prefer new grads that have relevant work experience, either as an intern or an employee.

Make a commitment to yourself to build your brand while you're in school. As they say, you're worth it. Continue to learn as much as you can about what employers in your field are looking for in new hires. Then find ways to provide the evidence that you can meet those needs.

During your job search, whether it's while you're in school, during your senior year, or after you graduate, you're going to be asking a lot of people for help. At different times, you'll be requesting networking contacts, resumé advice, and finally, you'll be asking for a job. Most people—especially your friends and family—want to help with your job search. However, no one can help unless you're clear about what you need. **The more focused your request, the more likely people are to respond.** If someone says, "I'd like to help you with your search," be sure to say, "As a matter of fact you can!" Instead of asking, "Do you know anyone who's hiring?" be specific: "I'm really interested in interactive marketing for a consumer products company. Do you know anyone at one of the firms here in town?"

Brand Strategy:
Start with your target customer and work backward. What does he need, and how can you show you can fill the need?

exploring values

Taco Bell thinks branding is so important that it's developed a training class for employees called Personal Branding. Erin Kappenberg, a trainer who facilitates the course, says that the process of creating a personal brand builds self-awareness and creates an emotional connection among participants. **She says your personal brand is a snapshot of the best things about you.** Your brand is a "statement of who you are and what you stand for. It's the essence of who you are." She says your brand can be the lens through which you make decisions, for yourself and for the company. Once they've created their brand statement, participants discuss how well they are communicating their brand and ways they can improve their impact on others.

Organizational Specialties

In Chapter 3, we discussed 10 industries and their cultures. Another way to think about where you might fit in the job market is to think about specialties within an organization. Whatever the industry, even in government and nonprofit sectors, most of these specialties exist. The size of the firm is a major factor in determining whether work is organized into specialties. Entrepreneurs often start with a few employees and slowly add more people when the volume of business justifies the additional cost. Initially, everyone pitches in and performs a variety of tasks. As the business grows, the need for structure and specialization increases.

Because this is how organizations are structured, employers are looking for people to fill openings in each specialty. **Employers expect you to know which specialty fits your skills and interests and why you've chosen to work in it**.

The most common specialties are listed in Activity 5.1. As you will see, each specialty adds value to an enterprise in distinctive ways. Each one solves different kinds of problems and faces different challenges. As you read about the specialties, pay attention to your reaction. What words appeal to you? What turns you off?

Preparing for a Specialty

You'll need more information in order to decide if a particular specialty is really the right one for you. Many of the same resources you found while researching industries will help you learn more about a specialty. You'll find that career sites on the Web, discussion groups, job descriptions, and articles in professional journals will provide a wealth of information about any specialty you're considering.

Specialties exist to meet an organizational need. You'll want to uncover enough information so you can decide if meeting this need seems like an interesting challenge to you. **Be sure to think like a futurist, and find information about how the specialty is likely to change**. Will it be meeting the same needs, or will it evolve into meeting new challenges? Many specialties are revamping to meet the demands of the new economy; the evolution of accounting that we described in the last chapter is just one example.

Here are some good questions to ask about specialties:

- What kind of person does well in this area?
- To succeed in this field, what skills should a person have?
- Am I working toward the right degree for this field?
- How do I see this field evolving in the future?

Yes, but I Want to Go into Management

Few firms today place new hires in management training programs. Large- and medium-sized organizations have leadership training programs geared to "high-potential" employees. Companies who provide this training are hoping to retain talented, committed employees. In addition, they often draw from this pool of employees to appoint team leaders as well as managers. However, you have to start somewhere, and that place is within a specialty that you feel passionate about. Once you've mastered a body of knowledge, you'll be ready for leadership, if that's your desire.

Organizational Specialties

Instructions: Read the descriptions carefully. Circle the specialties that appeal to you the most. Highlight the words within the descriptions that you find most appealing.

Specialty	Typical Activities
Finance	Manage the organization's money. Prepare and analyze financial reports, invest and borrow money for the company, and prepare budgets and balance sheets.
Administrative Services	Provide support services such as facilities management, security, and secretarial and administrative assistance.
Human Resources	Develop and implement systems and procedures to hire, train, promote, and evaluate employees. Write job descriptions, conduct salary surveys, and recommend salaries and benefits for each position. Forecast the labor pool needed to meet strategic plans. Train employees in classrooms and via e-learning.
Marketing	Enhance the organization's brand by planning and executing the conception, pricing, promotion, and distribution of products or services. Conduct market research, determine pricing strategies, plan promotions, and develop distribution channels.
Sales	Persuade potential customers to purchase products or services by building relationships with customers. In some companies, sales are directed to consumers; in others, they are directed to businesses. Sales administration, customer support, and supervising special accounts are other roles within the sales function.
Public Relations, Communication	Communicate with employees, stockholders, government, and the public. Write press releases and handle the media. Plan and execute events to promote the company and its products.
Information Systems	Operate and maintain an organization's computer system, including hardware and software. Manage information systems (like the Marketing Information System) that help managers make effective decisions. Advise management on technology purchases or design systems to capture the data needed to run the business efficiently. Maintain the company Web site(s).
Operations	Oversee the activities necessary to create products and services. Operations include the following functions: research and development, production planning, quality control, purchasing, inventory control, and scheduling production.

Once you've researched the specialty, review the values and skills you identified in Activity 1.1 in Chapter 1 and Activity 2.2 in Chapter 2. How well do your preferences fit the specialty? The following activity will help you analyze the information you've gathered.

Analyzing the Match

Instructions: After you've completed your research, answer the following questions. Then decide if you're on the right track or if you need to rethink your choice.

In which industry sectors have you identified the most positive characteristics with the fewest negatives? (Review your choices in Activity 3.2.)

....

....

....

....

Which specialties might be a good match for you? Consider your values and favorite skills.

....

....

....

....

Characteristics that appeal to me:	Characteristics that don't appeal to me:
....	....
....	....
....	....
....	....
....	....
....	....
....	....
....	....

Who can you talk to who would have the "inside scoop" on the industry sectors and organizational specialties that appeal to you?

....

....

....

....

Top 10 Demand Occupations—Why They May Not Matter

Most college students want to know the future demand for their career field. Many lists of "hot careers" are published every year. These projections are based on past statistical trends and the opinions of industry insiders—who always want their field to look promising, whether the facts bear it out or not. Often, they don't consider the impact of new technologies or the global economy. It's interesting to compare several lists and see how they differ. Remember, demand today is no guarantee for the future. Don't choose a career solely on projections, because they may change. Just ask the people who studied computer science in the 90s! Talking to people who work in the field can give you a more accurate picture of the demand for an occupation in your geographic area.

Don't dismiss a career option because demand seems low. Demand for specific skills is constantly changing. While the job market was flooded with IT experts during the 90s, now there is a shortage of skilled people in this field. People who choose occupations based on their passions and interests are usually able to discover a successful niche and develop winning strategies to achieve their dream.

Real Fact

There are no mistakes! Make the best decision you can based on the information you have at the time. So get the facts and decide well.

What If You Change Your Mind?

If you are a few years away from graduation, you are likely to discover new information as you take additional courses and learn about new career opportunities. As a result, you may decide that you want to take a second look at your career plan. That's OK—in fact, it's the right thing to do. For instance, in this course you are learning a good deal about what a career in marketing would be like. You may decide you're intrigued by the challenges and opportunities in this field. Taking additional courses in marketing will help confirm that choice—or change your mind.

Your experiences in various classes are a good barometer of future career satisfaction. If you enjoy learning about a subject, you're likely to enjoy work that is related to it. **Remember, your career plan should be flexible, and that sometimes means changing your goal**. Many college students feel pressure to choose a career and a major very early in their college days. That is understandable, considering the high cost of education. At the same time, don't discount your own reactions to information that you gather while you're in school.

So change your mind if a different field fits your personality and career goals better than your first choice. You might not have to change your major just because you change your career choice. Many successful people have college majors entirely unrelated to their career field. The important thing is to get a degree!

If you do change your goal, be sure you do the same thorough research we've been recommending throughout *Brand You.* You'll still need to develop your brand—it may require retooling your message for a different type of consumer, but it still needs to be done.

ACTIVITY 5.3

My Career Journal

What specialties interest you the most? Why?

_____

_____

_____

_____

_____

_____

_____

Reality check: Does the specialty you're considering match your values and skills? How?

_____

_____

_____

_____

_____

_____

_____

How do you think a personal brand can help you achieve your goals?

_____

_____

_____

_____

_____

_____

_____

Notes to **Myself**

6
Meeting Employers' Needs:
How the Selection Process Works

Objectives

1. How do employers decide whom to hire?

2. As a job candidate, what can I expect?

3. How can I decode a job description?

With your diploma in hand, you'll be seeking work in a world in which the amount of information available to make business decisions is exponential. There is a premium paid for employees who can sift through the data to make good decisions, often before all the relevant facts are in. It's all about response speed. It used to be that employers were looking for an extra pair of hands. Today, they seek *talent*, people who will contribute to the business innovations and new products the market demands. People who see themselves as talent are committed to high standards and staying current in their field. Talent is such a sought-after commodity that the head of human resources may now refer to herself as the VP of talent management.

People who purchase products and services are no longer customers, they're clients. The emphasis has shifted from single transactions with customers to relationship-building with clients. Employers want adaptable people who are willing to learn new skills and try out new ways of doing things. With so much attention paid to change and flexibility, there is a definite advantage to being a new college grad! True or not, young people are seen as more flexible and adaptable than their seniors.

In this chapter, we'll cut through the jargon and examine the personal characteristics employers are seeking right now. **You'll follow the employer's decision process and use a technique for finding the exact skills a particular employer is seeking.** In later chapters, we'll show you how to use that information to build your brand.

things new grads do better

1. Relate to college students
2. Travel
3. Perform routine tasks—they aren't boring yet
4. Spend more time researching and preparing for interviews
5. Provide a fresh perspective
6. Know the latest technology
7. Bring a flexible approach
8. Cost less
9. Show enthusiasm
10. Do activities others dislike

The Role of Human Resources in the Hiring Process

The size of the company has an impact on the role of human resources. Small companies probably don't even have a human resources specialist. The managers may do their own hiring, or the company may rely on head-hunters or recruiters to find employees for them. These recruiters make rec-ommendations (and earn a commission if their candidate is hired), but the final decision is up to the manager or owner of the company. Larger firms usually have human resource departments and strict hiring guidelines everyone follows. Often, human resource personnel will train managers in proper hiring techniques. These companies know that their reputation is determined in part by how it treats employees and job candidates. Many companies have learned that diversity is good business practice. And of course, they want to avoid discrimination lawsuits.

In the selection process, the human resources department doesn't say "yes," but it can say "no." **Often, when you meet company representatives on campus for the first time, you are meeting someone from the human resources department**.

Generally, human resources personnel screen resumés and send those that meet the job qualifications to the manager of the department in which the open-ing exists. They may also conduct a **screening interview**, either in person or over the phone. Human resources employees may not know the details of the job, but they understand the general requirements and are familiar with the job description. Human resources personnel are also very familiar with the corporate culture, and they often evaluate candidates through this lens. The more you know about the organization, the more you can discuss how your skills and personal characteristics would fit with their culture.

The hiring manager (the manager of the department in which you will work) makes the final decision. **This person is crucial to your success as a job hunter; consider their motivation as you develop your brand**. Figure 6.1 shows the hiring process. Notice that these are the same steps described as the Business Buying Process in *Marketing: Real People, Real Choices*.

Figure 6.1 The Hiring Process at a Glance

Problem Recognition

> The manager of the marketing department needs an assistant. She thinks about what the person will do and the skills needed.

Information Search

> HR reviews salaries in the local market, talks to marketing manager about qualifications, and posts ads on the company Web site, job boards, and newspapers. Manager asks around to see if anyone knows a good candidate.

Evaluation of Alternatives

> HR representative reviews resumés and may screen applicants by phone. She sends 10 resumés to marketing manager, who selects 6 people to interview. She may interview her top three choices a second time.

Selection

> Manager makes choice and notifies HR. References are checked and job is offered. Candidate accepts.

Postpurchase Evaluation

> New hire placed on probation. Manager decides she is happy with her choice and after six months, offers a permanent position.

How the Hiring Process Works

Interviewing for a professional position, an internship or entry-level job, is more involved than interviewing for a part-time job. Many companies interview candidates three or four times and may take several weeks to extend an offer.

1. **Screening interview.**   Your first interview may be over the phone with a recruiter from the human resources department. The purpose of this interview is to determine whether you meet the basic qualifications for the job. If you do, you will likely be asked to interview in person.

2. **Company-fit interview.**   The first in-person interview determines whether your personality, skills, and attitudes match the company culture. It may take place on campus or at the company's place of business. Usually, a recruiter or human resources representative conducts the interview and screens out candidates who don't seem to fit. For example, a company may be looking for people who work well in teams, deliver excellent customer service, or solve problems independently. **Successful candidates will be referred to the hiring manager**.

3. **Hiring manager interview.**   Your second in-person interview will probably be with the **hiring manager—the person for whom you will work**. Usually the hiring manager interviews 6 to 10 candidates to evaluate skills and experience related to the specific work that has to be done.

4. **Final selection interview.**   The top two or three candidates are sometimes asked to come back for another interview, which might be a panel of co-workers. **Making a good impression with the panel is just as important as impressing the manager**. Many managers will reject a candidate if co-workers don't think the person will fit in with the team.

Interviewing and selecting candidates is not a science. Sometimes you will be interviewed by experienced people who know how to make you comfortable and ask questions that bring out your best. You will also meet interviewers who are inexperienced and end up doing most of the talking. **Preparation and practice will help you find ways to interject relevant information to sell yourself**. If an interview goes poorly, it might have more to do with the interviewer than you.

Human resources professionals and hiring managers know that resumés and interviews are only two ways to evaluate candidates. Now that almost everyone has learned slick answers to tricky questions, many companies administer tests, request work samples, and examine portfolios.

Selection Tests

Many employers, ranging from consulting firms to manufacturers, use pre-employment tests to help decide which candidates to hire. Current estimates suggest that as many as 30 percent of *Fortune* 500 companies use some type of testing to match candidates to openings. The smaller the company, the less likely you will be tested.

In competitive fields, for which finding enough qualified candidates is difficult (health care, engineering, and technical positions), professional certification is used instead of testing. In industries in which customer service is critical (service firms, retail, and hospitality) the use of tests is increasing. You may not encounter pre-employment testing as a new college grad, but you are likely to face testing sometime during your career.

Testing is controversial. Because many people are concerned that tests are culturally biased, federal and state legislation has been enacted to ensure that tests are administered equally to all candidates. Any company using tests for selection must show that the criteria used to evaluate test results are relevant to the job.

Tests allow employers to ask more questions in a shorter amount of time and to ensure consistency among all applicants. **Several types of pre-employment tests are used: personality tests, task-oriented tests, problem-solving tests, and honesty tests**.

The goal of **personality tests** is to help identify candidates who match the corporate culture. Too often, people try to ace the test, but this may give a false impression. You may be doing yourself a disservice by presenting yourself inaccurately. If you present yourself as someone you are not, you may be selected for the position and find yourself in a job that doesn't fit your personality. The employer may, for example, expect you to be more outgoing than you are, if that's how you responded to the test. Honesty is the best policy. Be yourself and be realistic about your strengths. There are no right or wrong answers to the questions, so answer what is true for you regarding your beliefs and attitudes about work.

Task-oriented tests evaluate your technical knowledge and skills. You may be asked to demonstrate computer literacy, programming, or other technical skills required in the position. Your scores will be compared to those of employees working in the position. These scores are only part of the selection process. A company will often hire candidates with lower test scores if, overall, their response to questions is positive.

Problem-solving assessments present a variety of situations that the candidate may encounter on the job. You may be asked to role-play a situation (like dealing with a difficult customer) or solve a particular problem. Some companies use assessment centers, where an observer watches you complete a variety of tasks. In all these situations, your analysis of the problem and the way you go about solving it are more important than whether you arrive at a perfect solution.

Employers who hire people for work that involves direct access to money often administer **honesty tests** to help screen out applicants who may be dishonest. These multiple-choice tests ask the same questions several times to test the consistency of your answers and your honesty. They are often worded in a way that makes it sound as if everyone is dishonest. Don't be offended. There is no way to prepare for these tests. Just answer them truthfully.

 ## what do employers look for?

1. Communication skills (verbal and written)
2. Honesty/integrity
3. Teamwork skills (works well with others)
4. Interpersonal skills (relates well with others)
5. Strong work ethic
6. Motivation and initiative
7. Flexibility and adaptability
8. Analytical skills, solves problems well
9. Computer skills
10. Organizational skills

Demonstrating the Personal Characteristics Employers Want

An important aspect of building your brand is demonstrating the personal characteristics for which employers look. Following are 10 characteristics sought after in today's job market and some tips and suggestions from recruiters.

Communication

Interviewers look for written, verbal, and electronic communication skills. **Your resumé and cover letter demonstrate your writing ability**. The interview shows whether you can clearly express your ideas verbally. Speak like a professional. Know your industry, learn the right language, and use the right buzzwords. Don't use academic jargon and talk in generalities. Discover the key words and phrases used by insiders. If you don't understand what an interviewer is asking, don't be afraid to ask questions for clarification. It is much better to ask than to assume incorrectly.

Real Fact:
College helps you to expand the characteristics listed here. As CEO of Brand You, it's your job to provide the proof that you have them.

If you feel that you could improve your writing skills, make an appointment to go to the campus writing center. To be sure your interviewing skills are well honed, go to your campus career center and set up several mock interviews. It will be worth your time.

Honesty/Integrity

The recruiters we interviewed said that even if they don't ask direct questions about honesty, they rate candidates on ethics. If you can back up information on your resumé with more specific information, you'll be considered honest. **Some interviewers ask for examples of situations or projects in which you have faced personal dilemmas and then ask for details on how you handled the situation**. They look for the level of match between what you describe and what they would expect of an employee confronting a parallel situation. Most employers confirm dates, employers, and degrees listed on your resumé. Some employers conduct extensive background checks, including researching criminal records and credit ratings.

Teamwork

Most companies use teams to complete projects or solve problems. Whether they're looking for programmers, accountants, or customer service reps, they want people who can work with others. One manager told us, "I look for a person who can bring balance to our team. I discuss their skills and accomplishments to find what value they can add." **Describe how you participated in study groups, activity committees, and work teams**. What did you contribute? What was your role? What did you do to help the team stay focused on the task?

Skills

Do you get along with a variety of personality types? Do you adjust your communication style to that of other people? Do you resolve conflicts or create them? Saying you are a "people person" is not adequate. **Employers want work-related examples that show how you successfully worked with a difficult teammate or calmed an angry customer**.

Strong Work Ethic

Employers want workers who will do more than simply show up on time. They want employees who will complete their projects on time and care about the quality of their work. **Pointing out that you worked or completed an internship while attending school and/or maintained a high grade point average are great ways to show evidence of a strong work ethic**.

The Buzz

In a *Fast Company* interview Len Schlesinger, COO of Limited Brands said, "In interviewing potential hires, I look for passion first. Second, interpersonal sensitivity. . . Third, a willingness to articulate a point of view. I don't care whether it's right or wrong, but they do need to have one. Skills come after that. Always. You can always teach people the skills they need, but if they are a schmuck, they're a schmuck."

Motivation and Initiative

Employers want candidates who have demonstrated initiative by gaining experience in the industry while in college. **A recruiter for a *Fortune* 500 company told us that internships are key.** He doesn't consider candidates without intern or co-op experience. You can also show initiative in the interview by being prepared. Research the company and ask good questions. Show the interviewer that you have invested the time to learn about the company and this position.

Flexibility and Adaptability

Interviewers say flexibility is important in today's workplace as organizations continuously strive to improve the way they do things. **Share experiences that demonstrate your ability to manage change**—moving to a new city, changing colleges with good reason, adapting to a new boss, trying new approaches to solve a problem, and so on.

Analytical Skills, Solving Problems

As a knowledge worker, employers will expect you to be able to gather information through various media and keep it organized. People who are good analyzers know how to ask and answer the right questions, evaluate information, and apply this knowledge to workplace challenges. In many positions, you'll also need to use quantitative tools, such as statistics, graphs, or spreadsheets. No matter what industry or specialty you choose, you'll be involved in solving problems. **Be prepared to discuss how you go about identifying problems, develop a range of possible solutions, and then launch the solution.** Most of your college courses provide ample opportunity to apply these skills.

Computer Skills

No doubt there is a computer in your future—perhaps on your desk or in the palm of your hand. No matter what your major, you'd be wise to take a few computer courses, if needed, so you are **fluent with Microsoft Word, Excel, and PowerPoint**. Employers will also want you to write coherent and concise e-mail. Researching information on the employer's Web site will also be a key skill to develop.

Organizational Skills

With the premium on time so prevalent in today's workplace, being organized is a top priority. This means more than keeping your workspace neat, although that's one aspect. You'll need to organize and present information you've gathered about a topic in a logical sequence. You'll also need to organize multiple projects and meet every deadline. In today's workplace, multitasking rules!

If you feel like your organizational skills need improvement, check to see if your school offers time management seminars. You will be surprised at how much it will help you in all areas of your life.

Analyzing Your Strengths

Instructions: Look over the 10 characteristics just described as the ones employers look for in a job candidate. Then answer the questions below. You have ability in all these areas, but be honest with yourself. Everyone can improve.

Characteristics that are my strengths:

....
....
....
....

Characteristics I want to improve:

....
....
....
....

List below activities that will help you develop the characteristics you want to strengthen. Choose things you'll really do and keep your commitment to yourself.

....
....
....
....

Sample activities to strengthen your skills

Take a communication course	Volunteer for a community service organization
Work on a group project	Join a professional association as a student member
Join a campus club and run for an office	Travel to a foreign country
Take a speech course	Take computer courses
Make oral presentations in class	Take a creative- or business-writing course
Practice listening	Set a personal goal and achieve it
Work at a job that involves contact with the public	Invest in an electronic or paper organizer
Keep a journal	Take a research methods course
Take a time-management class	When you intern, ask if you can work on a team
Visit the writing center at your school	

Getting Down to Specifics

One of the best ways to determine the specific skills a particular employer is looking for is from the job description. Notices you see on the Web are a brief synopsis of the qualifications the company wants the candidate to have.

It's a good idea to explore various job descriptions now so you can prepare for the position you're likely to want in the future. **Highlight the employer's needs, including skills, and personal characteristics**. Skills are either action verbs or words that end in "ing." Characteristics are adjectives like detail-oriented or highly motivated. Chris decided to do that and here is one job description she found:

Marketing Assistant

We're Optibiz Corporation, a leading supplier of optics, photonics instruments and components, optomechanical components, positioning equipment, and vibration control. We are currently seeking a detail-oriented and highly motivated marketing assistant. Selected candidate will assist in the development and implementation of promotional marketing activities in our vibration control group. This will include: forecasting marketing trends of new/existing products; developing catalogs, brochures, and other collateral material; tracking and reporting advertising/collateral budget expenditures; implementing trade show efforts; and supporting product management processes. Requires a bachelor's degree in marketing or 3+ years applicable marketing experience. Knowledge of MS Excel is essential. Optibiz offers an excellent compensation and benefits package, a leading-edge work environment, and opportunities for professional growth. We invite qualified candidates to send or fax a resumé to. . . .

The next step is to create a plan for developing the required skills while you're in college. Here is Chris' plan.

Student Profile—Chris

Although this employer isn't in the consumer products industry, it is located in the city where Chris wants to live after graduation. After reading through this description and others, Chris made the following plan:

1. Obtain an internship in market research.
2. Take a course in graphic arts—Chris is more interested in writing, but she realizes it would be an asset to know the principles of good graphic design.
3. Start a subscription to Marketing News to study effective marketing techniques.
4. Become more proficient using Microsoft Excel.

ACTIVITY 6.2   ## Developing the Right Skills

Instructions: Visit a job board like www.monster.com, www.collegegrad.com or www.wetfeet.com. Find a job description that interests you. Highlight the skills and characteristics the employer is seeking. Write the skills and your development plan in the space below.

Skills listed in the ad:	My Development Plan

My Career Journal

Now that you've looked at some job descriptions that appeal to you, what do you like best about these kinds of work?

_____

_____

_____

_____

_____

How well do the skills in these job descriptions match the skills you like using (refer to Activity 2.2, Skills Inventory)?

_____

_____

_____

_____

_____

Review the list of 10 characteristics employers seek in this chapter. Which three are your strongest assets? What activities have you done that show these are your strongest skills? How can you capitalize on them as you market yourself? What are some specific tactics you can use?

_____

_____

_____

_____

_____

_____

_____

_____

_____

Notes to **Myself**

7

Sharpening Your Focus:
How to Use Target Marketing in Your Search for Work

Early in his senior year, Dennis Kruchek wisely started his search for work. Active in several campus organizations, he assumed his self-confidence, popularity, and the good sense of recruiters would help him land his first professional job. Dennis was sure that after talking to him, recruiters would know just where he would fit into their organization. Dennis signed up for fall interviews on campus. With resumé in hand, he talked to recruiters from many kinds of companies. He was enthusiastic about his abilities and Dennis let recruiters know he was open to considering whatever vacancies they had. When it was all over, Dennis was shocked when he didn't hear from recruiters again. What did Dennis do wrong?

Many job seekers approach their job search just like Dennis. Instead of targeting their search, they want to keep their options open. Perhaps, they reason, there's an employer or job out there that would be perfect. They're afraid they'll miss it if they target their search for work toward one segment of the job market. What these unfocused job seekers don't realize is that recruiters can't suggest additional options unless you can explain to them your strengths and the type of work that interests you. It's a fact—people who are unfocused have more difficulty finding work than someone who has a particular goal in mind.

One problem with an unfocused approach is that you lack direction. That makes it hard to know whom to contact or what to say once you do. Wal-Mart can have an undifferentiated market because it can afford mass media advertising. You, on the other hand, probably can't. Second, unless you

Objectives

1. Why should I target my job search?
2. How do I decide which segment of the job market to target?
3. How can I position my personal brand to influence potential employers?
4. How do I bring my personal brand to life?

tune in to the needs of a particular market segment, you won't know how to develop your own personal brand—a clear, consistent message about the value you have to offer. You won't know what to emphasize among all your skills, talents, and experiences. This makes it difficult to write a resumé or develop dynamic answers to interview questions.

Just as individuals are not all alike, neither are business consumers. As we've said many times, every business wants to hire employees who will create value and satisfy its particular needs. You'll find that using target marketing strategies will make your work search efforts easier, and you'll actually find a job more quickly.

Target Marketing

As you learned in *Marketing: Real People, Real Choices*, target marketing is necessary in today's world because people have diverse interests and backgrounds. Businesses are diverse, too. A high-tech manufacturer has very different reasons for forming an enterprise than a school, for instance. Instead of trying to sell your skills to everyone, it makes sense to target a particular segment of the job market.

Segmentation

Segmentation is the process of dividing the total market into different segments based on meaningful, shared characteristics. In the case of the job market, this segmentation has already been done for you. In Chapter 3, we called them "industry sectors," and described 10 different ones. Hopefully, you have researched these 10 sectors and decided which one(s) you prefer. Through your research, you should also know something about the sector's characteristics.

One way you can learn about the characteristics of a sector is by studying the corporate cultures of companies within that sector. As we saw in Chapter 3, usually there is quite a bit of similarity among firms in one sector. Articles in trade magazines and professional journals often describe the interests and motivations of organizations.

The table on the next page compares a few of the characteristics of the education sector and the high-tech-industry sector. These two sectors have different interests, although of course, both want to achieve their missions. Therefore, they have different needs they want employees to fulfill. When you compare sectors in this way, you can see the difference in the way you would want to develop your brand, depending on which type of employer you are targeting.

Education Sector	High-Tech-Industry Sector
Use communication skills	Use analytical skills
Provide learning opportunities	Provide solutions to problems
Values doing good for society	Values innovation, speed to market
Values expertise	Values customer/supplier relationships
Motivated by ideals	Motivated by achievement
Expects compassion	Expects results

ACTIVITY 7.1 Characteristics of My Preferred Sector

Instructions: Place the name of your preferred industry sector in the top row of the box below. Then list all the characteristics you've learned about that sector from your research. Consider their business interests, organizational culture, and their needs.

Sector that interests me:

You may be considering more than one sector at this point. If so, complete the box below in the same way. Comparing the differences will help you prioritize your choice.

Sector that interests me:

Targeting

Targeting
Evaluate the sectors, and then choose the one that's right for you.

Targeting is the process of evaluating the attractiveness of each potential segment and deciding which of these groups is worth spending resources on to turn into a customer. The group becomes the **target market**. In your search for work, you will be using resources too—your time and energy. Zeroing in on a target allows you to put your resources where they'll have the greatest effect. **You can have more than one target market, but you'll want to fine-tune your messages (your resumé, cover letter, and interview responses) to appeal to each market.**

Here are some questions to help you evaluate industry sectors:

- Why does this sector appeal to you?
- Do your values match the values of the companies in this sector?
- Is the sector large enough, that is, are there enough potential employers?
- Do companies in this sector exist in the geographical area where you want to live? If not, are you willing to move to a different location?
- Do you have the knowledge to serve the market?
- Do you have the expertise and experience they seek? If not, do you have the means and motivation to acquire it (through coursework, internships, or other activities) before you graduate?
- The bottom line: Is this a realistic target?

Developing Sector Profiles

Use a Concentrated Marketing Strategy:
Focus your efforts on a single sector so you can effectively appeal to the needs of that segment.

It is helpful to generate a profile of "typical" companies in the sector that you want to target. This is a more detailed look than the previous exercise, in which you were looking at the characteristics of an industry sector. In this phase, you are drilling down to really understand the companies within the sector in which you might want to work. This profile will really help you zoom into the organizations' needs and look for employment opportunities. **Within a sector, you may be interested in several subgroups.** For example, within the manufacturing sector, you might be interested in high tech, aerospace, and pharmaceuticals. In that case, you should develop a profile for each group or segment.

Chris, the marketing student we've been following, decided to write a profile of consumer products companies. Her description highlights the characteristics of the firms she researched. She wrote down what she thinks they are looking for in employees. She also created a list of potential employers and wrote down the demographic information (size of the firm, number of employees, location, and number of marketing employees) she thought would be useful when she started searching for work.

Student Profile—Chris

Chris decided to target consumer products firms in northeastern United States with $10 million or more in annual sales.

Chris' preferences: products that appeal to age group 18–25. Possible products: athletic clothing, cosmetics, health or fitness products.

Company characteristics: strong brand strategies, conduct extensive market research, emphasize supply chain management, and customer relationship management. All have Web sites to educate consumers; some not very effective.

Employers are looking for: people who can speak to young adults, stay current on market trends, analyze research data, have innovative ideas, work on project teams, know about brand management, and interact well with people.

ACTIVITY 7.2

Company Profile

Instructions: Research a handful of companies in the industry sector you are considering. List demographic information (domestic or multinational, location, number of employees, total sales), their needs, and the type of skills they are looking for. The more detailed the information, the more this profile will help you when you develop your resumé.

Type of company that interests me:

Company demographics:

Employers are looking for:

Company names:

Choosing a Targeting Strategy

Target for Success:
If you want to target more than one sector, write a different cover letter for companies in each sector.

Should you go after one sector or several? That depends. How sure are you about the sector you've selected? How large is the segment? If your first choice seems to have plenty of potential employers, one sector is all you need. However, if there are few employers in your geographic area, you may want to look at several types of firms within the sector, as Chris did. **If you decide you want to target more than one sector, write a profile for each sector**.

Your best chance for success is to use a concentrated marketing strategy. That is, you'll develop your own personal brand and marketing campaign to appeal to one or two segments of the marketplace.

As you become more adept as a job hunter, you can also take a customized approach. **This involves reworking your resumé, cover letter, and interview responses toward a specific company**. Remember how in the last chapter we looked at job descriptions, and highlighted the skills and knowledge the employer was seeking? Once you have a basic resumé, it isn't difficult to tweak it to meet the specific needs of one employer. We'll discuss this in more detail in later chapters when we talk about resumés and cover letters.

Positioning

The more you can position yourself as a person who can provide the skills and competencies that meet an employer's unique needs, the better your chances for being hired. **Positioning is developing a marketing strategy aimed at influencing the person who makes hiring decisions**. To do this, you'll first show how you can add value and satisfy their needs. Then you'll decide the best way to get in touch with the person who has the power to hire you. In the next few chapters, we'll show you exactly how to position your own personal brand.

Evaluating your own personal brand and the way you've positioned it is important. Once you've developed your marketing materials (your resumé and cover letters), evaluate the response you're getting from employers. The purpose of a resumé is to get requests for an interview. If it isn't doing that, you may need a different strategy for contacting employers, or a more effective cover letter and resumé.

Bringing Your Personal Brand to Life

Brands come to life and gain appeal when they seem to have a personality. Marketers do this by creating an image that captures the brand's characteristics and benefits. The image is more than a logo—it's the total impression that will be communicated in every phase of the marketing process. (If you doubt that brands have personality, think about the difference between the Geico gecko and the AFLAC duck.)

To bring your product to life, you don't have to start from scratch like a product marketer does—you already have a personality! Think of your personality as a cluster of characteristics that describe you. We think we know our personality, but sometimes other people are actually better at defining who we are. So to identify your personality characteristics, think about how people you know have described you. Would they say you're outgoing, influencing, and goal-directed? Or perhaps reserved, thoughtful, and thorough in the way that you approach tasks is a better way to describe yourself? The first cluster of characteristics is valuable in positions for which team interaction, leadership, or customer service is important. The second cluster is valuable in positions for which attention to detail, analyzing information, or implementing new ideas is important. In addition, consider how you typically react in various situations. For instance, do you tend to finish one thing before you start another, or do you like to have a variety of things on your plate?

When developing your personal brand, you want to build on your personality, rather than invent a new one. A helpful way to do this is to create a list of personality traits and adjectives you want to incorporate into your brand. You're looking for an identity for the product (you) and you want to show it to your target market. This identity includes the image you want to present, your personality characteristics, your skills, and behaviors that demonstrate what you can accomplish. These things, taken together, are what make you unique; they are the things you'll want to emphasize as you communicate your own personal brand to others.

If you're reading the advice from the Real People profiled in *Brand You*, you'll notice that several of them talk about the importance of showing passion in the interview. It's hard to show passion if you're hiding your true personality or trying to invent a new one. It's also hard to show passion if you haven't thought about your values and what is important to you. In creating your own personal brand, you are trying to identify who you are, so that you can find employment that is consistent with your values. When you know who you are and what you want, it's easy to show passion in an interview. **The right attitude to have during a job interview is "Here I am, here is what I stand for. Here is what I care about. If you want someone like me, I'm ready!"**

In the earlier chapter on research, we discussed the benefits of talking to people who work in the field to find out about employers' needs and exactly what professionals do. This is one of the best strategies you can use to bring your personal brand to life. Ask professionals about the specific characteristics employers in this sector look for in job candidates. Armed with this information, you can develop a brand that excites employers!

My Career Journal

Bring your own personal brand to life. List your personality characteristics that appeal to your target market. Don't try to be someone you're not!

_____

_____

_____

_____

_____

_____

_____

_____

How will your personality add value? What do you want to say about yourself when you are job hunting?

_____

_____

_____

_____

After talking with several friends and acquaintances, write down the five words people use to describe you.

_____

_____

_____

_____

Is there anything you'd like to change about the impression you make? What would you change?

_____

_____

_____

_____

Notes to **Myself**

Step 3 Creating Your Value Proposition

What do you have to offer to a prospective employer? How do you stand out among all the other students and graduates competing for an internship or full-time job?

Before you begin to write your resumé and cover letter, you need to clearly outline what you have to offer to prospective employers. **Step 3—Creating Your Value Proposition** helps you define what you have to offer to employers and what makes you unique. Chapters 8–11 include information, activities, and insights about how to translate your experience, skills, and passions into a concise statement about your value. And, you will learn how to use your value proposition to get the internship or full-time job you want or pursue an alternative career choice such as freelancing, contract, or other flexible work arrangements.

Your value proposition can also help you define your market value or how much you can expect to get paid for your internship or full-time job. You'll find out about the latest in salary trends and resources to learn about up-to-the-minute changes in the market.

Increase your value and you will increase your income. ➤

8
Creating the Product—You:
Identifying Your Value

If you've held part-time jobs during the school year or during summer vacations, you may think job hunting is no big deal. If your jobs have been in retail as a part-time clerk, or in the service industry as a server of some kind, your view is pretty accurate. You may have seen a sign in the window, gone in without an appointment, and filled out a job application. A few days later, you were called for an interview, answered a few questions, and were offered the job. It may even have seemed like they would hire anyone, as long as the person was breathing! In these kinds of low-wage jobs with high turnover, that scenario is often typical. Getting your first internship or professional job as a college graduate will be a different experience, however.

During your internship and postcollege work search, you'll be competing with other qualified students, new grads, and experienced pros. To be successful, you must compete at the same level as the pros do. You will need a professional image, a spotless resumé, and dynamic responses to interview questions. Seeing yourself as a tangible product can help you prepare for each step of the job search process. **Using the concept of product layers can help you sort through your preparations so they seem less overwhelming**.

The marketing adage cited in *Marketing: Real People, Real Choices* that states, **"A marketer may make and sell a ½" drill bit, but a customer buys a ½" hole" is a good metaphor to keep in mind as you develop your brand**. Your skills, knowledge, and experience are your tools—the drill that enables you to perform various tasks. The results you achieve are the benefits of those features—the ½" hole. You have many skills and a great deal of knowledge, but employers buy results—the value you can add to their organization.

Objectives

1. How can product layering help you define your strength?

2. How can you uncover the benefits you have to offer?

3. How can you design a professional package?

The work you'll be doing in this chapter includes essential steps you will use later to develop your value proposition. In this chapter, you'll learn exactly how to identify and describe the benefits an employer can expect from you and your work. You'll also decide the features you want to emphasize to employers.

You already have most of the information you need. You've evaluated your talents, strengths, and skills on the key dimensions employers seek. You've researched industry sectors and companies within those sectors to gain insider knowledge about the characteristics for success. With this information, you're ready to identify your product layers.

fresh ideas

You're spending time on-line anyway, why not leverage it? Try one or more of the ideas below, and then mention your achievements on your resumé. You can also describe your contributions and provide samples during an interview. Activities like these demonstrate your initiative, a quality employers are always looking for.

- **Contribute to an on-line brain trust** such as Lilly company's InnoCentive, Inc., It's a network community of 80,000 independent, self-selected "solvers" who tackle research problems for firms like Boeing, DuPont, and 30 other large companies. Drew Buschhorn, a 21-year-old chemistry grad student at the University of Indiana, participated. He came up with an art-restoration chemical—a compound he identified while helping his mother dye cloth when he was a kid. The "seeker" company paid Drew for his efforts. Says InnoCentive Chairman Darren J. Carroll, "We're trying for the democratization of science."

- **Create digital content** such as contributing to game production for Linden Lab's Second Life, where participants create just about everything from characters to buildings.

- **Create market buzz** such as contributing ideas for new product designs or participating in marketing efforts. Lego fans designed the new Santa Fe Super Chief train set. In less than two weeks, 10,000 units sold out, without other marketing. In Dallas, music fans volunteer to create buzz and build audiences for local bands through the local social network, Buzz-Oven. Like Mike Ziemer, you might start as a volunteer and end up working for the network.

- **Contribute to forecasts** such as those developed by NewsFutures, Inc., a consultancy that predicts profits and sales by creating on-line groups and running prediction markets for companies and publications.

- **Participate in open-source development** such as SugarCRM, Inc., which provides an open-source version of customer-relationship management software. Or consider SpikeSource, Inc., a start-up providing bundles of open-source products of all kinds.

- **Write buyers' guides and lists of favorite products** for Amazon.com and other e-retailers.
- **Blog for business.** You can contract with interesting companies to develop a blog on the company Web site that creates buzz for their products and their brand. Or, you might try maintaining your own blog for consumers, perhaps even acquiring sponsorship income.
- **Blog for a job.** Develop a social network for job-hunting students at your campus. Provide leadership and space for people to share networking ideas, discuss job-search strategies, and vent frustrations. Your blog will generate lots of ideas and one just might lead to the perfect job for you!
- **Join a Professional Social Network.** Create a profile, make connections and request introductions at professional social networks such as **www.linkedin.com** and **www.ryze.com**.

Defining Your Product Layers

Think of yourself as a bundle of attributes that includes the benefits, features, packaging, and supporting features of your product. In developing a compelling brand, you want to consider your total package—everything an employer will receive when she hires you. The three product layers are a helpful way to see yourself. Defining each of these layers, as they relate to your job performance, will help you develop your value proposition.

Figure 8.1 shows how a marketing major could adapt the concept of marketing layers to describe herself. **No matter what field you plan to enter, it's a good idea to define your own product layers**. One benefit of this illustration is that you can see the salient features and benefits you want to emphasize during your search for work.

The Core Product—Your Benefits

The core product consists of all the benefits you can provide for your customer. Because you have many skills, a wealth of knowledge, and a history of diverse experiences, you can provide many benefits to employers. But as we've said all along, the key to exciting your customers is to zoom in on those benefits that will add value to their enterprise.

Defining benefits is a little more difficult than identifying features (your skills and knowledge). **Benefits are the outcomes or results that occur because of your efforts**. Examples of benefits are higher sales, increased customer satisfaction, improved brand recognition, lower costs, and higher profits. Activity 8.1 will help you pinpoint the benefits you can provide that focus on an employer's needs. These benefits will become critical elements of your value proposition. Knowing the key benefits of your skills and knowledge is the secret to communicating effectively, whether you want to interview for a job or write a dynamic resumé.

Figure 8.1 Sample Product Layers for a Marketing Major

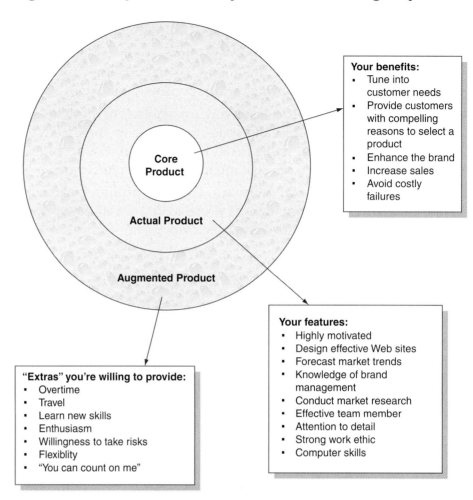

Your benefits:
- Tune into customer needs
- Provide customers with compelling reasons to select a product
- Enhance the brand
- Increase sales
- Avoid costly failures

Your features:
- Highly motivated
- Design effective Web sites
- Forecast market trends
- Knowledge of brand management
- Conduct market research
- Effective team member
- Attention to detail
- Strong work ethic
- Computer skills

"Extras" you're willing to provide:
- Overtime
- Travel
- Learn new skills
- Enthusiasm
- Willingness to take risks
- Flexiblity
- "You can count on me"

Hint: It will be easier to figure out your benefits after you write down your features.

The Actual Product—Your Features

People buy products and services to receive benefits. But the product or service has to *do* something in order for you to get the benefit. Even when you buy a necklace or a tattoo there is a benefit and some features. The benefit of your purchase is "bling" (or that's what you hope). The feature—its function—is to decorate your body. Of course, your customer, your next employer, won't be buying bling—she wants the genuine product, someone who can function and achieve results. Before they hire you, your customers want to know what you can *do*.

In Fact, the Most Important Thing You Can Do to Develop Your Brand and Plan Your Career Launch Is to Identify Your Features and Benefits

Just as a brand manager knows the product inside and out and decides which features and benefits to promote, you will be much farther ahead if you know yourself and your outstanding strengths.

Most of us take our strengths, talents, and skills for granted, which is why it isn't easy to identify them. However, once you know your strengths—that is, the skills you like using, the things you are good at—it will be much easier to know the profession or industry in which you fit best.

While you are in college you will be introduced to many learning experiences that are excellent ways to assess your strengths. *And* you'll have to spend time developing skills that you don't particularly like or are particularly good at. This is actually good information for you—your college experiences will help you decide if the assessment you are doing now is on target.

Build on Your Strengths

Don't worry about what other people think you should be good at or what you wish you were good at. Make enjoyment the criterion you use to decide which skills belong in your actual product.

Get Feedback

Most people think they know what they're good at, but they're not always right. It's important to get feedback on your strengths. How do others see you? Are their perceptions about your abilities the same as yours? If anything, most people tend to underestimate their abilities, so it's good to get other viewpoints. Get a reality check by asking people for their opinions (even if they're not your biggest fans). Anyone who knows how you tend to react to different situations can provide important insights. Some possible sources: professors, roommates, classmates (especially if you've worked on a project together), club members, parents, relatives, and if you've held jobs or internships, people with whom you've worked. Here are some questions you can ask them:

- What do you see as my major strengths?
- If you had a problem, what kind of advice would you ask me for?
- Under what circumstances do you think I work best?
- What do you think someone else would say about me?
- How can I improve how others see me?

Your actual product is the work you deliver that supplies the desired benefits. Remember, however, you are a total package, not just the work you perform. In addition to your skills, potential employers will evaluate your attitudes, your promises, and your presentation.

Attitude One attitude employers seek is a person who is committed to his career and to quality job performance. If you've done your homework by researching the company and its products, mission, and culture, you'll be able to convey that you're a determined candidate who takes her job search seriously. You can do this by discussing what you've learned about the company and how your skills match their needs.

Before you go on a job interview, put yourself in the shoes of the employer. If you were recruiting someone for this position, what attitudes do you think would be important? For instance, many employers focus a good deal of attention on customer service. In an interview, you could discuss ways in which you'll put the customer first. Other attitudes that might be important: self-confidence, flexibility, a willingness to take on new tasks, a commitment to producing top-quality work, and a desire to continue learning. **After you've identified attitudes that are important to the employers you'll meet, think of things you've done—actions you've taken—that demonstrate those attitudes.** There's a place for these actions on your resume and in the job interview.

Promises   Your own personal brand will have little meaning if you can't deliver the goods you promised in your interview. **This is a key reason why you should never over-promise or exaggerate your abilities.**

Presentation   Another major aspect of your package is how you present yourself when job hunting and meeting people. **Your transition from student to careerist requires more than trading in your backpack for a briefcase.** Your first real impression will likely be made in the first few seconds—right about the time you say, "My name is. . . ."

Looking professional takes preparation. Here's the scoop:

- Dress in business attire for interviews. You only have one chance to make a good first impression.
- When in doubt, choose a conservative look. You can't go wrong with neutral colors such as gray, black, or navy. Your clothes don't have to be expensive, but they should fit well.
- Pay attention to details. Scuffed shoes won't cut it.
- Women should avoid too much makeup. Bright over-outlined lips and dark-lined eyes should definitely be avoided.
- Body piercings are better left at home.
- The eyes have it—make eye contact with everyone with whom you interview.
- Leave cell phones and pagers turned off and out of sight.
- The perfect accessory is a smile—for everyone you encounter, not just the interviewer.

Managing the Product—You:
Launching and Managing Your Career

What's the difference between launching a career and managing it? Your career launch begins when you choose a career direction and follow it. Career management, on the other hand, is the ongoing planning and development of your career.

Managing your career is making choices along the way—deciding whether it's better to move from one industry to another doing the same work, or deciding to move up and learning how to accomplish it. It may involve new career choices, or it may involve developing new skills for the same employer. Either way, managing your career is continuing to choose the path you want to follow as you evolve, grow, and discover new opportunities. **Although your immediate concern is launching your career, over your lifetime, you'll return many times to these career-planning skills so you can move on to the next leg of your journey.** In this chapter, we'll discuss strategies for your launch and ways to manage your career. Let's begin by discussing ways to launch your career.

Objectives

1. What are the best strategies for launching a career?

2. How do I develop my value proposition?

3. How can an internship benefit my career launch?

4. How do I manage my career?

Real Fact:
Study after study in the last 30 years has shown that up to 80 percent of people in new positions found them through networking.

Strategies for Launching a Great Career

By completing the activities in this book, you're following a proven method for launching your career. Your reward will be fulfilling work and the motivation to perform well. You'll look forward to each new day, knowing your work will make a difference to your organization and your customers.

Have a clear objective in mind. Your career objective should first be based on your values—what *you* want to get out of your hard work. It should also take into consideration the skills you enjoy using and the type of environment in which you want to work. Finally, it should include the industry sector and specialty that interests you most.

Target employers that meet your objective.   Once you have a clear objective, research companies and talk to professionals to find employers who meet your criteria and need your skills. Your research should include finding out about the organizational culture of the firms you've selected.

Learn your targeted employers' needs.   Employers have needs to fulfill and problems to solve. Learn what they are so you can demonstrate that your skills and knowledge will solve their problems.

Develop your product.   Provide the proof that you can solve employer problems by completing the NAB process (see Chapter 13). Show how your education, past experience, and campus or volunteer activities relate to the skills that employers seek. Be sure to identify the results and benefits of your actions. Bring your product to life by developing a compelling value proposition.

Communicate your value proposition.   Using the information you've gathered about your customers' needs and your ability to solve their problems, you'll be able to develop a dynamic resumé and memorable responses to interview questions. You'll also be able to reach the people in your target market who have the power to hire you by using a variety of job-search techniques.

Now it's time to develop your value proposition.

Your Value Proposition—The Key to Success

As a working adult, you'll be asked many times to explain what you do. Whether you are job hunting, looking for an internship, networking at a professional association meeting, or trying to find a new project at work, your value proposition is the perfect answer to any inquiry about what you do.

Eighty percent of jobs are never listed—80 percent! That means they are found through personal connections and networking. In Chapter 14 you'll learn how to use the power of networking to find potential employers and great work. For now, realize that anytime you are introducing yourself to a potential contact or employer, your goal is to get the person interested in you. **Think of your value proposition as a 30-second commercial, with you as the product.** What makes you remember a great commercial? It's snappy, relates to your needs or wants, and makes its point.

⊘Launch Your Career with Marketable Skills

A college degree isn't the only ticket you're likely to need to launch your career. **Many recruiters say they don't interview students who haven't shown the effort to get real-world experience through internships, service learning, or cooperative learning programs.**

Internships

No question about it—internships provide opportunities to gain valuable work-related experience. It's also a great way for you to explore the real work world and decide if this truly is the career for you. With an internship, you are enhancing your academic education with practical career-related experience. The result? Marketable skills on your resumé.

Recently, Vault.com reported that in a survey of over 1,000 college seniors nationwide, 86 percent had completed one internship and 69 percent had completed two or more. **With so many students taking advantage of this resource, people without relevant internship or work experience are at a distinct disadvantage.** The numbers also suggest that obtaining an internship at a prestigious firm is a competitive venture. As internships become more and more competitive, it becomes even more important for you to have a strong set of job-search skills.

Your first step is to decide what you hope to gain from an internship. You might want an internship to help you evaluate your career goal, learn new skills to beef up your resumé, gain networking connections, or all of these. Knowing what you want to accomplish will help you evaluate internship offers. Inevitably, you'll be asked about your goals when you interview. Once you know your purpose, decide where you'd like to do your internship—what industry and specialty would best meet your needs?

The best time to apply for spring and summer internships is in the fall. Your freshman year isn't too soon to start. For more information about getting an internship, see Internships 101 in the *Brand You* Toolkit.

⊘**THESE SITES:**
www.quintcareers.com
www.wetfeet.com
www.internweb.com
www.vault.com
www.InternshipPrograms.com

Internships Work

"We always select and offer first from our pool of co-ops and interns, then from candidates that have worked during school to earn 50 percent of their way. We have found no correlation between GPA and subsequent performance, but have consistently found a substantial correlation between co-op/intern experiences and performance in the first five years." Staffing Recruiter, *Fortune* 100 Company.

creative ways to obtain marketable skills—student views

- "Foreign exchange programs. Study history in London for a semester or go to a foreign country to practice a new language."
- "Join a campus club, like the sociology or advertising club. An opportunity to network, develop skills, and make connections in school that could lead to work."
- "Enter your artwork for recognition and awards. When you win, it reinforces that you're good and keeps you going. It's a good opportunity to practice new software applications."
- "Complete a project during your internship. Have something concrete to show for your work, like a brochure or a report."

Manage Your Career by Remaining Employable

Career-Management Strategies

- Be resilient.
- Develop flexible plans.
- Expand self-awareness.
- Think like a futurist.
- Communicate your value.
- Be ready for the next opportunity.

Keeping one's career alive by remaining employable has become *the* critical mission for every working adult. As Jason Averbook, a senior manager at PeopleSoft warns, "Time-to-market for new products and services has shrunk dramatically over the past 10 years. Employee skills are now outdated in three to five years, and new jobs will emerge (each year) that involve tasks that don't even exist today."

No matter where you are working, following the Career-Management Strategies (shown in the margin) will ensure that you succeed in today's workplace. As CEO of your own personal brand, plan on using these strategies to thrive in the workplace. By doing so, changing work demands won't leave you stranded, wondering where your next paycheck is coming from.

Be Resilient

As you learned in *Marketing: Real People, Real Choices*, products reach a peak and then sales start to decline. Marketers use a number of strategies to lengthen the product life cycle as much as possible. A similar phenomenon happens to careers.

Figure 9.1 shows the progression of one's career over time. For most people, their productivity and value to an organization rises in the growth stage of their career. After they reach a peak, productivity begins to fall. This drop can occur because the job becomes routine. More often in today's world, it occurs because the person doesn't keep growing and learning to stay current with new ideas and/or technology. As a result, his value to the organization drops dramatically.

Figure 9.1 The Career-Resiliency Concept

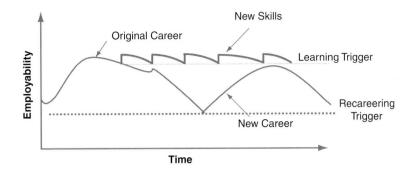

Almost everyone can sense when his productivity is falling—he feels bored, dissatisfied, or burned out. Left untended, these feelings worsen, and the person usually ends up recareering, sometimes by his own choice and sometimes because he is terminated.

Instead of denying these feelings of dissatisfaction, resilient careerists use the information as a trigger to take action. They know they are responsible for keeping their skills up-to-date. They actively seek new opportunities to stretch their comfort zone by taking on new projects. They continuously learn through company-sponsored training, coursework, professional associations, and reading books and journals.

Resilient people are proactive. They take charge of their careers and make sure they have choices. That way they can bounce back from the impact of changes in the marketplace.

Develop a Flexible Career Plan

Although we can't know exactly what the future holds, we can create flexible plans that allow for uncertainty. **Plan your career to keep up with continuous changes in the world of work.** A flexible plan helps you set targets for achievements and also allows you to take advantage of emerging opportunities. As you add new skills to your portfolio, you'll be ready for challenges you couldn't imagine when you launched your career. Many successful people are surprised by their achievements—they didn't necessarily aspire to their current role. Their success occurred because they kept on learning and were willing to take risks when opportunity came knocking.

As we mentioned earlier, five years is about the right length of time to look ahead for your career plan. As you approach that milestone, use the same process you've learned here and set new goals for the next three to five years.

Expand Self-Awareness

By following the steps to develop your career plan, you've seen that the cornerstone of good planning is awareness of your strengths and preferences. As you gain different experiences, learn new skills, and acquire new knowledge you will develop into a person who can readily handle responsibilities you can barely imagine today.

Most working adults know that in the future we will have five to seven careers. Many people are alarmed by this fact. They think it means they will be adrift in a sea of change without a life preserver. **However, you'll always have a lifeline—your skills and knowledge.** Most of your career changes will be incremental rather than disruptive. The more likely scenario is that you will reconfigure your skills to meet new needs in the marketplace. Rather than moving from banker to physicist, it will look more like an engineer moving into technical sales or a marketing analyst moving into brand management.

Look inside yourself to focus on what you want to do next. It will be a necessity to keep pace with changes in the marketplace. **Periodically take an inventory of your updated skills and preferences and map out new territory for your own personal brand—just as you are doing now.** Recognizing that you have choices will give you the self-confidence to adapt to change.

Think Like a Futurist

Continually scan the work environment to discover emerging trends and needs. **When you hear about an interesting new trend, think about the impact it will have in the marketplace.** You'll discover new opportunities that will keep you interested and engaged. Just as a product gains market share through early arrival into the marketplace, you'll gain prominence in your profession by becoming an early adopter of new career trends.

Your future promises to hold unprecedented opportunities. As CEO of your own personal brand it's your job to study the future and prepare your business for tomorrow.

Communicate Your Value

Marketing *you* is a never-ending process. Keep an eye on the next big work project, company shift, or product innovation, and position yourself to participate in completing the task(s). That means being able to sell yourself.

Once inside a company, learn what the organization values. Ask to see the strategic plan. Look for ways to align your work with your employer's strategic goals. Anticipate the skills that will be relevant in the future and map out a strategy to develop them.

Look for ways to gain visibility in the organization. Volunteer for special projects and problem-solving teams. Find a mentor who will help position you for new assignments. Use e-mail to send progress reports to your manager and other key people in the organization. Volunteer for community service projects sponsored by the company. One team leader told us, "I volunteer for our corporate sponsorship with Habitat for Humanity. The person next to me pounding nails might be a VP, and I wouldn't even know it unless I asked."

Real-Life Perspective

Josh Williams works as the training manager for an insurance company. In six years the company has merged four times. After the most recent merger, Josh investigated the values of the new owners and adjusted his duties to fit their priorities. He doesn't like all the changes, but he still has his job. Meanwhile, 27 of the department's 30 employees have been laid off.

Be Ready for the Next Opportunity

Once you're in the workplace and performing your best, you will see new opportunities. So you always want to be prepared. That means tracking your accomplishments and keeping your resumé current.

Sharpen your job-hunting skills so you can change your position or your career when you're ready for the next opportunity. **One way to keep your value proposition fresh is to join a professional association.** You'll always be meeting new people and telling them what you do. Not only will these contacts help you find new opportunities, the experience of talking about your accomplishments will make job hunting less intimidating.

ACTIVITY 9.2   # My Career Journal

Take a look at the Value Proposition you developed in Activity 9.1. How could you change it for a gathering held by a professional organization?

_____

_____

_____

_____

_____

_____

How could you change it for a career fair?

_____

_____

_____

_____

_____

Think of some companies or job settings that might be of interest to you in seeking an internship either during the summer or during the school year.

_____

_____

_____

_____

_____

_____

_____

_____

Notes to **Myself**

10
Providing Services as Brand You:
Exploring Alternative Ways to Work

One of the exciting advantages of the twenty-first century is the wide variety of working relationships that you can choose. Until a few years ago, there were really only two options for nonagricultural workers—shift work or full-time salaried positions. Today, many options exist: temp workers, contingent workers, contractors, free agents, entrepreneurs, job sharers, and consultants. Each of these options appeals to people because they offer lifestyle flexibility and perhaps higher incomes than could be expected from a single employer.

When you choose one of these options, you have a lot in common with marketers of intangible goods and services as described in *Marketing: Real People, Real Choices.* **Presentation of a "total package" is very important!** Differentiating yourself from the competition by highlighting your tangible qualities—appearance, speech, knowledge of company, industry, and/or product—can set you apart and start you on the ideal career path for you.

Alma Garcia thought she was living her dream. With a marketing degree from the University of Illinois, she moved to New York, started moving up in the marketing department at her new job, and was making good money. There was only one problem; she was miserable. Up at 6 AM, she would get home just in time to watch the late-night news; she also often worked weekends. "I reached burn out pretty quickly," says the 27-year old, who yearned for some time for herself. She found it when she moved back to her small Illinois hometown and started her own marketing firm. Now she has plenty of time to enjoy sports, volunteer at a women's shelter, and enjoy her friends and family.

Objectives

1. How can I achieve work/life balance?

2. What if life in a large corporation isn't for me?

3. What are alternative ways to earn a living?

4. How do I "blaze a trail to success" with my own personal brand?

Corporate life is not for everyone. In today's highly competitive environment, corporate employees frequently work over 40 hours per week, often placing a strain on family life. Parents worry about what their children are doing while they're at work. Rather than succumb to corporate pressures to perform, you may prefer a simpler lifestyle that provides more balance between work, family, and leisure.

This chapter discusses alternative ways of working and examines the advantages and disadvantages of each. **If you're unsure whether you want to join the corporate world, perhaps it's time to think about other ways of working.** You just may find an alternative that matches your personality and lifestyle preferences.

The number of people working in alternative arrangements has increased dramatically in recent years. Many people started doing so after being laid off, and then found they preferred their new lifestyle. Other people become disenchanted with large companies when their boss wouldn't accept their ideas for improvement or they were passed over for a promotion. These are realities that frequently occur when you work for someone else.

Many experts are predicting that everyone's work life will be more flexible in the future. Many of us will move from entrepreneurship to full-time jobs in corporations to consulting, and back, full circle. If you are truly in charge of your career, you can leverage many different types of opportunities when they arise. **Of course, to manage this type of career successfully, thinking of yourself as your own personal brand is imperative.**

Myth or Reality?

For generations the prevailing advice for young adults was to "settle down and get a good, steady job." This advice wasn't voiced by mean, uncaring adults. It was the economic imperative of the time. Income statistics proved it was right year after year. In those days, striking out on your own was simply not a viable option for most people.

This conventional wisdom became so entrenched that it is still the basis of many assumptions about the job market today. Assumptions act as filters that affect the information we gather and the way we evaluate it. Assumptions and beliefs can continue to influence decisions even when they are no longer true. Most schools still dismiss students in June, even though children no longer spend summers helping out on the family farm.

Outdated assumptions limit possibilities and impact the way you think about your future. If you're like most people, you may have difficulty separating myth from reality. Without realizing it, you may be relying on outdated advice as you plan your future. Check the advice you've heard against the following facts.

Myth: Company loyalty is rewarded with job security and a secure retirement.

Reality: Job security is a thing of the past. Career savvy employees create financial security by choosing projects and opportunities to help them stay in demand as employees. People who continually develop new skills in their professions and seek new work opportunities earn more than their counterparts who remain loyal to one company.

Myth: A college degree guarantees a good job.

Reality: A college degree doesn't come with any guarantees (sorry). A recent business school graduate was complaining that even though the employment rate was improving, she'd had no luck finding a professional job. When asked about the focus of her job search, she responded, "Oh, whatever, I just want to get my foot in the door." When asked if she had developed professional relationships or contacts while in school, she replied, "Not really—I was too busy studying." When asked about relevant work experience or internships, she had none.

Myth: The best jobs are in large corporations.

Reality: Large companies used to offer more advantages, including job security and career advancement opportunities, than small companies. That gap is narrowing. Since 1980, the proportion of the American workforce employed by *Fortune* 500 companies has shrunk significantly. Some of the best opportunities are in small companies. The real growth and opportunities for rapid advancement will come from microbusinesses (those started with fewer than four employees), venture capital–backed start-ups and entrepreneurial-venture start-ups within large companies.

Myth: Go to work for a good company and move up the career ladder.

Reality: In the past, Americans worked for large companies, in which they had opportunities to move up and build careers over a span of 20 or 30 years. New college graduates entered management training programs and followed predictable career paths, with periodic promotions. The career ladders are gone. **Today, the responsibility for career advancement and employability has shifted from the company to the employee.** Although companies may offer assistance through tuition reimbursement and training programs, the clear message is that you are responsible for developing your own career path, including finding ways to identify and learn the skills you'll need for continued employment.

The Changing Workplace

Not only have the sheer numbers of companies in the United States increased significantly, but the ways employees contract their services to employers have also increased. Some professionals choose one of these options. Others fall into it when they cannot find suitable full-time work. Out of necessity many people have tried these new approaches to get work and now they wouldn't trade them for traditional employment. These new ways of working provide more autonomy and more variety. Keeping track of your intangible skills and qualities is imperative. Many individuals who want continuous employment put more faith in their own marketing ability than in the vacillations of corporate payrolls. Here's a look at some of the new work options that are available.

Core employee. Permanent employees are being referred to as *core employees*. The number of core employees is shrinking as companies increase their reliance on other hiring options. Companies retain core employees whose work is directly involved in the design, testing, production, and distribution of core products. Support and staff positions such as customer service, communications, shipping, product repair, human resources, and accounting are outsourced to smaller firms or "offshored" to cheaper workers in foreign countries.

Contingent worker. Companies hire additional people during peak periods, so the number of employees is contingent upon the amount of work that needs to be done. When the peak period ends, these workers are off to another gig (think movie productions). Entertainment companies are not the only ones who rely on contingent workers—many manufacturers do when they're ramping up a new product. Companies who need seasonal workers, such as hotels and retail stores, also hire contingent workers. All types of nonpermanent employment—such as contract, temporary, and part-time work fall into this category. Contingent workers may contract directly with employers or they may be paid through a temporary agency, a contractor, or a consulting firm.

Concurrent worker. Working two or more different careers at the same time is called concurrent work. An example is the computer programmer who writes code on a flex schedule that allows him to spend evenings and weekends pursuing his career as a rock musician.

Indie. Pro sports figures aren't the only ones who consider themselves free agents or independent contractors. Indie includes production designer, photographer, event planner, and offers the ability to choose your own clients. These are highly skilled freelance workers who are loyal to their profession rather than to a particular employer. Indies look for interesting and challenging work that allows them the freedom to use their knowledge and provides opportunities to improve their skills.

Job sharer. Sometimes the best person for the job is actually two people for the price of one. The advantage to the employer—there are two minds instead of one. The advantage to the job sharers—they can choose the part-time work schedule that suits them best. Job sharers include positions such as receptionist, medical assistant, customer service, and human resources.

On-call worker. On-call workers are called into work when needed and aren't guaranteed a set number of hours. Many health care workers, repair technicians, and even wildfire fighters work on call.

There used to be a sharp division between self-employment and working for someone else. As these alternatives show, these distinctions are increasingly blurred. Indies and contractors may work for one client organization for several months or even years. Are they self-employed or nonpermanent employees? Perhaps it depends on perception. But more likely, it depends on the worker's career goals. Some people take contract positions as a way into a company in which they want to work. **Contractors who see themselves as self-employed keep their options open by networking and marketing, no matter how long a project lasts.**

Trends Driving Alternative Work Options

Affordable Technology

New technology is putting powerful tools once available only to large organizations into the hands of people who are using them to start home-based and other small businesses. Today, with computer and telecommunications technology, we can work virtually from anywhere—in cities, small towns, suburbs, even hilltops, or seaside cabins. For a small investment anyone can have the same capability as a *Fortune* 500 company.

Outsourcing

Organizations have become leaner (and more economical) by sticking to their core business. Support departments are disappearing as companies outsource necessary but peripheral tasks. Because of technology, it's often more cost effective for big business to contract with individuals and small firms than it is to hire employees. Outsourcing is so prevalent that even CEOs are working on contract! These turnaround specialists take on ailing companies, improve their financial operations, and then move on to the next needy client.

- "Working as a consultant, you have to do your own marketing—that means that you have to allot time to that process as well as put on a different mind-set. I personally found that very hard work. I also had to deal with the natural feelings of rejection when speaking to potential clients who didn't buy my services."
- "I must say that I like it. Money and a certain amount of freedom."
- "Typically, there is more variety in assignments."
- "You can have more flexibility in your schedule."
- "There are no buddies to meet in the hallway or bounce an idea off of. I've got a network of folks to call now, but it takes a while to set that up."
- "I personally have to discipline myself to get dressed before I go to my basement office, or I find myself in front of my computer at 3:00 PM still in my jammies!"
- "Companies expect you to be at your best at all times, no ups and downs, because they are paying you premium bucks to be the best. You need to guard your emotions and mood swings so that you are always professional and prepared."
- "Autonomous freedom is wonderful—especially if your previous experience was being micromanaged. On the other hand, you may (and probably will) find yourself working much harder and for longer hours than you ever did for someone else."

Small-Business Services

As the number of small businesses increases, so does the need for services to this sector of the economy. Service businesses are the fastest-growing sector in our economy. They mainly serve other small businesses by meeting essential needs like accounting, marketing, desktop publishing, Web site maintenance, and newsletters.

Niche Consumer Markets

From nannies to personal shoppers, people are creating niche markets of people-based services to meet the needs of busy two-career couples and single parents. Increasingly pressed for time, consumers need other people to take care of the ordinary chores of living, such as housecleaning, running errands, taking care of pets, and home improvement.

Choosing Alternative Work Styles

When you work for someone else, you have a safety net. Although you don't have a guaranteed job, you do have access to benefits and retirement plans. Your work is usually well defined and predictable. You also have support from co-workers and the satisfaction of inclusion in the organization's community. So why do people choose alternative work styles? Here are some of the reasons they cite:

- More control over their work life. People can choose their clients, schedule, and tasks.
- Combine earning a living and a simpler lifestyle. With telecommunications and computer technology, many young professionals are opting to live in small towns or rural communities.
- See direct results of their efforts. These workers enjoy developing relationships with clients and seeing the results.
- Freedom to do the work they love. In corporations, most professionals spend countless hours in meetings and other required tasks. The self-employed aren't impeded by company politics, bureaucratic systems, or mercurial bosses.
- Greater opportunities for women and minorities. Small business is often the place for these individuals to find respect and fair compensation for their skills.

Preparing for Going Solo

✅ Enroll in entrepreneurship courses while you're in college. This is one way to assess your interest as well as to prepare for the realities of setting up shop.

✅ Develop a business plan.

✅ Recognize that you'll have to get really good at marketing—and that it will be an ever-present part of your work life.

✅ You don't have to be a risk-taker (although it helps), but you do have to be self-managing.

✅ Great interpersonal skills are a must. You'll need referrals from clients to succeed and that will happen only if you can establish positive relationships (and keep your commitments).

ACTIVITY 10.3   ## My Career Journal

Do you see yourself working in a "typical" 9:00 to 5:00 job, or launching an alternative career path upon graduation?

_____
_____
_____

If you would prefer the security and camaraderie of being a core employee, what steps can you take now to achieve that status?

_____
_____
_____
_____

If you would prefer the freedom and uniqueness of an alternative career, what steps can you take now to hone your skills and/or make contacts with others involved in the same type of work?

_____
_____
_____
_____
_____
_____

Notes to **Myself**

11

Pricing the Product:
What Salary Can You Expect?

In the general marketplace, price is the value that customers exchange to obtain a desired product. In the job market, your price is usually a salary. It's the amount of compensation (including benefits and other perks) an employer is willing to give in exchange for your valuable skills.

Employers, like all consumers, have expectations about what a product (you) is worth. Salaries fluctuate in the same ways as product pricing. Competition, demand, revenues, and the environment impact the salary you can expect. Just as marketers try to come as close to "reasonable" as possible when deciding on price, your chances of obtaining work increase when you set reasonable salary expectations. In this chapter, you'll learn how.

You'll be happy to know that 80 percent of the time when people negotiate salary, they are successful. This doesn't mean they always get everything they ask for, but it does mean they get more than they were originally offered.

Objectives

1. What salary can I expect?
2. How do I determine how much it will cost me to live in a particular city?
3. How can I increase my value?

How Do Employers Decide on a Salary Range?

Employers are expert talent consumers—they analyze the bottom-line contribution of a position, research the job market, and determine a salary range. For most positions, the range varies by just a few thousand dollars. The top of the range is reserved for experienced pros—entry-level employees earn at the lower end of the scale.

Employers conduct research to determine the range they will offer to job applicants. They look at pay ranges for their industry, and also examine salaries for the same position in other industries in their geographical area. Many salaries vary by region because certain major cities, such as New York, Washington, DC, San Francisco, and Chicago, for example, have higher living expenses than other regions. They also consider the unemployment rate, availability of qualified applicants, economic outlook, and the desirability of their company as an employer. It's no wonder that after all this research and analysis, most employers are quite firm in adhering to the salary range they've set, especially for entry-level positions.

How Demand Influences Salaries

Salaries fluctuate with demand. **When demand is high (employers need you), then salaries rise.** Availability of skilled employees is the factor that has the most impact on demand. When there are not enough skilled workers available to work in an industry or profession, then demand for those employees increases. Companies increase the salary and/or benefits they offer to job candidates in an effort to entice them to come to work for them. **On the other hand, when the economy slows down, demand for employees decreases.** When the unemployment rate is high, many people are willing to accept lower salaries—it's almost always better than unemployment compensation!

Progress in technology also impacts demand. When a new technology is adopted by businesses, employees are needed who can operate, maintain, or service it. Think of all the IT positions that have been created with the introduction of computers and software. Demand is usually highest the first few years after a new technology is adopted. College students and unhappy workers hear about the new opportunities and rush to acquire the education and training needed to enter the new field. Sometimes so many people seek this new work that almost overnight too many employees are available.

The perceived value of a profession is another influence on salary. Each enterprise values (and compensates) its core employees the most. Core employees contribute directly to the bottom line and keep the engine of commerce running. The perception of who is a significant contributor varies according to the type of industry. Manufacturers value their engineers and scientists, while law firms prize their attorneys. A company's business model also influences the perceived value of professionals. One business may place a premium on finance experts, while another may esteem its marketing gurus.

New consumer needs also create demand. For example, the baby boom generation is reaching retirement age. In 2006, each day 8,000 boomers

Communicating Your Value Proposition

Think of your favorite ad. Think about what makes it great...it is the right message for the right product at the right time in the right place?

Now think about your personal brand. Will your advertising be as compelling?

Yes, it will!

Chapters 12–14 will give you the framework to create an integrated marketing communications plan for your brand and powerful advertising (resume and cover letter) that will help you get interviews at the companies that are on the top of your target list.

Don't make the mistake of only sending out a few resumes to see what response you get. Use the activities and resources in Chapters 12–14 to actually implement your "advertising campaign" by getting out your cover letters and resumes on-line and off-line. There is no single answer for the best way to get out your cover letter and resume. But like successful brands, you should use all (not just some) of the methods available to you. Prospective employers can't hire you if they don't know about you.

You're in charge of your career. Get the word out about your brand. ➤

12
Creating Your Communication Plan:
Getting the Word Out about Your Brand

Objectives

1. What is the best way to make my brand stand out when I apply for internships or full-time jobs?

2. What are the most effective tips for sending my resumé to target companies?

3. Are career fairs really worth it?

4. What else can I do to let people know that I am looking for an internship or a job?

5. How can follow-up make my brand stand out in the crowd?

Now that you have defined your brand, it's time to craft your own **integrated marketing communication (IMC)** plan. Think about great brands like McDonald's, Coke, and Verizon. Each of these brands communicates often (you see each ad multiple times), uses multiple media at the same time (TV, magazine, radio, Internet, etc.), and tailors their message for the different segments of their target audience (for example, McDonald's has ads that market salads to health-conscious women, premium sandwiches to working professionals, and Happy Meals to moms and children).

You want to follow the same strategy whether you are looking for an internship or your first full-time job. Think of your cover letter and resume as "advertising" for your brand. You want as many people in your target audience to see it as frequently as possible. You many also want to tailor your cover letter for each segment of your target audience. You'll learn how to do this in Chapter 13.

Your Integrated Marketing Communication Plan

As part of your IMC, you will use media mix or a mix of different ways to reach your target audience. In Chapter 4 you learned about resources to use to conduct your research. Now you will learn about the following seven "media" you can use to effectively get your resume to the right people at the right time:

- On-line job boards and recruiting Web sites
- Social networking Web sites
- Company Web sites
- Direct mail
- Career fairs
- Networking
- Follow-up

Increase your chances of getting the internship or full-time job you want by using all of the options you have to get the word out about your brand. You will only get a response from a small percentage of resumes you send out using any of these "media." Use all of these options frequently to increase your chances of success. Don't make the mistake of only using one or two "media." Give yourself every opportunity to have multiple job offers from which to choose. You can get the job offer you want if you use all of the following "media" in your integrated marketing communication plan.

On-line Job Boards and Recruiting Sites

On-line job boards and recruiting sites should be an ongoing part of your integrated marketing communication plan. There are hundreds of Web sites that have job listings in a variety of industries. These are all internships and jobs that are currently open, and the listings are updated daily in most cases.

You should consider using a combination of many Web sites. The most popular job boards are important since they have the largest number of jobs. But don't limit yourself to only those sites. There are many sites that have unique listings or aggregate job postings, provide excellent search tools, offer e-mail alerts and have career planning information.

Since job sites are powered by search tools, it's important to use the right keywords. Make a list of keywords to use in your searches on these sites so that your searches yield relevant job results. You will only see the jobs you want if you take the time to create comprehensive searches with the right keywords.

If you want to post your resume to a job site, take a minute to read the privacy policy of the Web site to be sure your contact information will be protected. Based on the site's privacy policy you may want to skip posting your resume and only use the site to search and apply for jobs.

Activity 12.1 will guide you as you create your own list of Web sites you will use for your work search. It's a good idea to review the Recommended

Keywords Are Key

Maximize your relevant results on job boards by generating a list of keywords for use on each Web site. For example, if you are looking for an entry-level account management position in an advertising agency, your keyword list might include advertising, agency, account management, client services, coordinator, specialist, marketing, interactive, and account coordinator.

Privacy, Please

Before you post your resume to a job bank, read the privacy policy of the Web site. If you want to post your resume to the site, be sure it allows you to limit your name and contact information to be private. Resumes with contact information that are posted on the Web may be at risk for identity theft.

Get the Skinny
Read the Do's and Don'ts of
On-line Job Searching in the
Brand You Toolkit.

Web Sites list in the *Brand You* Toolkit. Don't forget to include local job boards and local professional organizations on your list. Here are some ideas about how you can identify the best on-line job sites for you.

- **General job boards and recruiting sites.** Web sites like **www.monster .com**, **www.careerbuilder.com**, **www.wetfeet.com**, and **www.experience .com** are great places to start. See the Recommended Web Sites in the *Brand You* Toolkit.

- **Job boards and recruiting sites that specialize in your target industry.** For example, if you are looking for a job in Internet marketing, Web sites like **www.marketingsherpa.com** and **www.sempo.org** are excellent resources. See a list of recommended Web sites by industry/specialty in the Recommended Web Sites in the *Brand You* Toolkit.

- **National, regional, and local professional organizations in your target industry.** Professional associations such as American Institute of Certified Public Accountants, American Marketing Association, Public Relations Society of American, and others are ideal places to search for information and job postings. A list of key professional organizations is included in Recommended Web Sites in the *Brand You* Toolkit. Or, go to **www.associationjobboard.com** to find the national associations in your discipline. In addition, research local trade associations such as the local advertising club. Most professional organizations have job listings on their Web sites.

- **National, regional, and local trade publications that serve your target industry.** Go to the Web sites of the publications that serve the industry in which you are interested. Most trade publications also include jobs on their Web sites. If you don't know the name of any trade publications, ask one of your professors. He or she will be happy to give you the names of the best trade publications in your target industry.

In addition, many trade publications have a regular e-mail newsletter. This is an excellent way to stay abreast of news in the industry. And, many trade publications also offer a hard-copy magazine at no charge to subscribers.

Social Networking Web Sites

**Social Networking
Works**
Join professional social networking Web sites to establish
connections in your target
industry.

www.linkedin.com
www.ryze.com
www.jobster.com

You are probably comfortable using social Web sites for communication with your friends and classmates. Many companies use sites such as Facebook and MySpace to recruit for internships and entry-level jobs.

In addition, professional social networking Web sites such as **www .linkedin.com**, **www.jobster.com**, and **www.ryze.com** can help you develop contacts in your target industry and/or at your target companies. Most professional social networking Web sites provide the option for you to create a profile/resume and many also include a job board. Linkedin.com offers a feature called Jobs Insider which is linked to several of the major job boards and shows you the names of people in your network who work for the hiring company. You can request an introduction to the hiring manager at the company. Social networking combined with personal networking (discussed in Chapter 14) can be an extremely effective way to create and develop professional relationships.

A word of caution about social networking and job searching...you are available to prospective employers 24/7 on-line. **Be sure your pages, blogs, pictures, videos, and all other communication on ALL social networking pages are appropriate for prospective employers to read at any time.** Don't assume that prospective employers won't search the social networking Web sites to see who you are and how you express yourself. Take the time to review your pages to be sure everything you have posted is appropriate and is an accurate reflection of you.

Company Web sites

Companies constantly post open positions on their Web sites. And, many companies do not use job boards or recruiters. Don't just rely on job boards to learn about open positions. Here are some tips about how to use company Web sites in your job search.

- **Visit Web sites for companies in your target industry.** In Activity 12.1, you will create a list of at least 25 target companies for which you would like to work. To create your list, you will use the research methods you learned in Chapter 4. You may want to review Chapter 4 as you are preparing your list. Here are a few reminders of resources you can use to identify your target companies:

  ○ Use the professional and trade publication Web sites as well as **www.bizjournals.com**, **www.hoovers.com**, **www.yellowpages.com**, and the business section of the local city newspaper or newspaper Web site to find the names of local companies in your industry or specialty.

  ○ Another good source for company names is the list of 100 Fastest Growing Companies. Since these companies are growing, they are usually hiring people. The Web site of the local major city newspaper or **www.bizjournals.com** will have a listing of local and/or regional fastest growing companies. National business publications such as *BusinessWeek* and *Fortune* publish the national/international lists.

  ○ Other lists published by local and national business publications could also be helpful such as the Top Public Accounting Firms, Top Public Relations Agencies, Top Advertising Agencies, Top Interactive Marketing Agencies, Top Investment Banking Firms, Top Financial Services Firms, Best Companies to Work For, America's Most Admired Companies, Best Employers for New Grads, Top Companies for Women, Top Companies for Minorities, Top Companies for Leaders, Top Places to Start Your Career, Top Companies for Families, *Fortune* 500, Global 500.

    If you are looking for local business lists such as these, go to **www.bizjournals.com** or the Web site of your local city newspaper. If you are

24/7 Branding
You are always marketing your personal brand whether you realize it or not. Be sure your on-line blogs, pictures, videos, and social networking pages are appropriate for prospective employer viewing.

Check It Out
Use the Recommended Web Sites in the *Brand You* Toolkit to start complete Activity 12.1. It will give you some ideas about where you can find your target companies.

Find the Best Companies

Business lists are an excellent source to help identify target companies. The list of fastest growing companies in your city is an excellent place to start. Go to **www.bizjournals .com** to find business lists for your city.

looking for national and international business lists, go to the Web sites of business publications such as **www.wsj.com**, **www.businessweek .com**, **www.money.cnn.com/magazines/fortune/**, as well as national trade publications such as *Advertising Age* at **www.adage.com**.

Your target company list should include professional services companies (such as advertising agencies if you want to go into advertising or accounting firms if you want to pursue a career in accounting, etc.) as well as companies that may a have a department in your target area. For example, if you want to go into finance, identify companies that have a finance department.

○ Business directories such as *Advertising Red Books*, *Directory of Corporate Affiliations*, and others can also help provide information about companies and agencies by geography and type. Many business directories are available on-line and at no charge in your campus library.

Let's look at a list that Lauren Knight compiled. Lauren is a marketing major who wants to pursue a job in advertising in the Philadelphia area. She completed Activity 12.1 My Target Web Site List by using the research resources covered in Chapter 4 and highlighted here. She also used the Recommended Web Sites included in the *Brand You* Toolkit. And she met with her professors, the librarian, and a counselor at the campus career center.

• For General Job Boards and Recruiting Web sites and Industry-Specific Job Boards and Recruiting Web sites, she researched the Web sites included in the Recommended Web Sites list in the *Brand You* Toolkit. and went to her campus career center and found out about some local job boards and industry-specific job boards.

• For Professional Organizations and Web Sites, Lauren is a student member of the American Marketing Association so she added that to her list. She learned about the other professional organizations from her professor including the Philly Ad Club.

She was pleased to find the Philly Ad Club Web site which includes a directory of hundreds of advertising agencies in the area in addition to a job board, news, and events. She added it to her list and is now planning on attending the next meeting.

• She asked her professor which business and trade publications were best, so she added all of them to her list. Her professor also recommended the *Philadelphia Business Journal*. She also went to the library to find some of the business lists mentioned above. The librarian showed her how to get the business lists that were compiled by the *Philadelphia Business Journal*. He also suggested she use the *Advertising Red Book* since it lists advertising agencies, company information and key management names for each agency by city.

• She used the business lists from the *Philadelphia Business Journal*, a list of advertising agencies from the *Advertising Red Book*, and added some companies that were listed at the campus career center and some she had read about in the area to create her list of target company names and Web sites.

Following is the list Lauren complied for Activity 12.1. Her target company list actually included 26 companies; all are not shown here.

Lauren's Target Web Site List

General Job Boards and Recruiting Web Sites	Industry-specific Job Boards and Recruiting Web Sites	Professional Organizations and Web Sites	Trade Publications, Directories, and Web Sites	Target Company Names and Web Sites (Grouped by type)
Monster monster.com	Marketing Jobs marketingjobs.com	American Association of Advertising Agencies aaaa.com	*Advertising Age* adage.com	**Advertising Agencies** The Brownstein Group brownstein.com
Yahoo! Hot Jobs hotjobs.yahoo.com	Marketing Sherpa marketingsherpa.com	American Advertising Federation aaf.com	*Brand Week* brandweek.com	LevLane Advertising & PR levlane.com
Career Builder careerbuilder.com	Talent Zoo talentzoo.com	American Marketing Association ama.com	*PROMO* promo.com	1 Trick Pony 1trickpony.com
collegegrad.com	The Creative Group creativegroup.com	Direct Marketing Association dma.com	*Ad Week* adweek.com	160over90 160over90.com
indeed.com	Aquent aquent.com	Search Engine Marketing Professional Organization sempo.org	*Direct* direct.com	**Packaged Goods and Food Companies** Campbell Soup Company campbells.com
The Vault vault.com	The Boss Group thebossgroup.com	Philadelphia Ad Club phillyadclub.com	*Philadelphia Business Journal* pbj.com	Tasty Baking Company tastykake.com
Philly Jobs phillyjobs.com			*Advertising Red Book* redbooks.com	Rita's Water Ice ritaswaterice.com
South Jersey Jobs southjerseyjobs.com				**Retail Companies** Urban Outfitters.com urbanoutfitters.com
Campus career Web site				Charming Shoppes charmingshoppes.com
				The Pep Boys pepboys.com
				Five Below fivebelow.com

My Target Web Site List

Instructions: Choose a specific industry in which you are interested, and then list the Web sites that you will use in each of the categories below. Complete a new chart for each industry you wish to pursue. Be sure to include local job boards and local professional organizations on your list. You may find it helpful to create your list in Word or Excel using the format below. Bookmark these Web sites on your computer so you use them frequently.

General Job Web Sites	Industry-specific Job Web Sites	Professional Organizations and Web Sites	Trade Publications, Directories, and Web Sites	Target Company Names and Web Sites (Group by Type)

Here are some tips to help you maximize your results from applying for internships or jobs on-line:

- **Sign up for job alerts or job agents.** Whenever possible, use these tools to alert you to new jobs that are open.

- **Search Web sites regularly.** If a Web site does not offer job alerts, search the Web site at least three times every week for new jobs.

- **Search synonyms or similar words.** If you are interested in marketing, you can search for marketing, but also search for sales, promotion, advertising, interactive marketing, advertising agency, account executive, account coordinator, marketing specialist, or other marketing words that would be used to list marketing jobs.

- **Apply for jobs as soon as you find them.** Keep in mind that there are many other people who are applying for the same job.

- **Include your cover letter. Always** include a cover letter with your resume when you apply for a job. A short e-mail note is not enough to set your brand apart.

- **Personalize your cover letter.** If a person's name is listed in the contact information, address your letter to "Dear Mr. Jones," or "Dear Ms. Jones," If the person's name is not listed, address your letter to "Dear Sir or Madam," or "Dear Employer,".

- **Tailor your cover letter to the job.** Incorporate key aspects of your experience that reflect the job requirements. There's more information about how to do this in Chapter 13.

- **Save your resume in multiple formats.** Microsoft Word is the standard format for all business communication. If you are sending your resume to an individual e-mail address, attach your resume in **Word** format. However, many job sites do not maintain the formatting of your resume if it is submitted as a Word document. For job sites, it is best to submit your resume in **PDF** or **plain text**. This will ensure that your resume will be easy for the viewer to read.

- **Save your resume as a PDF file.** You can convert a Microsoft Word document to PDF using Acrobat 9 Standard or Acrobat 9 Pro or visit **www.acrobat.com** and click on "Create PDF."

- **Save your resume as a plain text document.** (In Word, use File, Save As, then choose Plain Text in the Save As Type drop-down box.) Be sure to review your resume in plain text before you save it as you may need to make some modifications and delete some symbols that didn't translate. The plain text version can be submitted to those job sites that don't accept PDF.

- **If you are using Word 2007,** save the documents as Word 97–2003 documents to ensure that the recipient can open them. Don't forget to spell check your cover letter and resume before you submit them on-line.

E-mail Alerts

Set up e-mail alerts on job boards, and recruiter and company Web sites whenever possible so you don't miss any new jobs.

Keep It Fresh

Always look for new job boards, recruiter, and company Web sites to add to your target list. New Web sites can give you a fresh perspective on your work search.

Which Format Is Best?

Microsoft Word is the standard format in business communication. However, when submitting a cover letter and resume to an on-line job board, submit them in PDF or as plain text files to preserve formatting.

If you are creating your cover letter and resume in Word 2007, save them as a Word 97–2003 Document to ensure that all recipients can open them.

- **Double check before you submit.** Take one minute before you submit to reread your cover letter and resume to be sure spelling and grammar are accurate, the greeting is correct, date is correct, and any references to the company name are correct. This quick double-check can make the difference between your cover letter and resume getting noticed or getting discarded.

Don't stop here! As we said, Web sites are only part of your integrated marketing communication plan. If you want results, read on.

Direct Mail

One of the best ways to let prospective employers know about you and your value proposition is to send them a letter. Just like retailers who send you a catalog to showcase their new product lines, a cover letter and resume can communicate your skills to the right person at a target company...even before a job is open or posted. Not all companies post open internships or full-time jobs on-line, so a letter is the perfect way to let a prospective employer know you are in the market. **And, a hard copy letter can make you stand out and break through the on-line clutter.**

Keep in mind that direct mail usually yields a response of 1–2 percent, so it's best to send letters to as many target companies as possible. Send letters to all 25 of the companies on your target company list.

You should plan to send out at least 50 letters or more in each mailing (at least 2 to each company). You may want to do a few different mailings. For example, if you are targeting the public relations industry, you should have one mailing targeted to public relations and advertising agencies, one to companies with a public relations department, one to recruiting firms, etc. Use the company groupings you created in Activity 12.1.

To ensure success from your mailing, follow these key guidelines:

- **Send by mail, not e-mail.** Always send a cover letter and resume on paper via the U.S. mail. An unsolicited resume that is sent by e-mail is usually deleted.
- **Paper matters.** Use white or off white resume paper for both cover letter and resume. Choose 24-lb. paper (you can find it at your bookstore or office supply store or Web site).
- **Personalize your cover letter.** Address all envelopes and cover letters to a person in a department at a company (e.g. Ms. Kim Lu, Director of Finance, Home Depot). **Do not** send cover letters and resumes addressed only to a department or to a company as they will most likely end up in the trash (e.g. Finance Department at Home Depot).
- **Send cover letters and resumes to the right people.** Send a letter to the hiring managers such as the vice president, director, and manager of the department in which you would like to work as well as the vice president, director, and recruiting manager in Human Resources.
- **Send multiple cover letters and resumes to each company.** Send a cover letter and resume to as many **appropriate** people as possible in

each company. This will increase your chances for a response. You can send the same letter to each person, just be sure that each letter is individually addressed. (People do not compare letters, but they might pass them along to the appropriate person.)

Now that you have the big picture, you are ready to put together your mailings.

- **Create your mailing list.** The list of companies you created in Activity 12.1 is the basis of your mailing list of key people to whom you will send your cover letter and resume.

    Go to each company's Web site (or call the company) to find the name of the key decision makers to whom you will send your resume. Common titles of key people are

    - Vice president of the department in which you would like to work
    - Director of the department in which you would like to work
    - Manager of the department in which you would like to work
    - Account directors in professional services firms such as advertising agencies
    - Vice president of Human Resources
    - Director of Human Resources
    - Recruiting manager
    - Campus relations or internship manager (for internships)

Another good source for names and companies is local business and trade publications. Regularly read the articles that include the names and titles of people who have been promoted to a key position. Include them in your mailing list.

Be sure to spell all names correctly and use the formal name of the company in the address (e.g., Campbell Soup Company, not Campbell's).

Don't forget to send your resume to major recruiting firms that specialize in filling temporary and full-time entry-level positions such as Robert Half for finance and accounting jobs (**www.roberthalf.com**), Aquent for marketing jobs (**www.aquent.com**), Manpower (**www.manpower.com**), and Kelly Services (**www.kellyservices.com**).

See the Sample Company Mailing List at the end of this chapter.

ACTIVITY 12.2   Creating Your Mailing Lists

Build your mailing list in an Excel spreadsheet or a table in Word using one column for each piece of information (one column for Mr. or Ms., one column for first name, one column for last name, etc.). See the Sample Company Mailing List at the end of this chapter. Use a different spreadsheet or document for each mailing so that you can target your cover letter appropriately. Include phone numbers and e-mail addresses when you are conducting your research as that information will be helpful when you are doing follow-up.

- **Purchase your supplies.** Now that you know how many letters you will be sending, you should buy enough resume paper (two sheets for each letter), envelopes, paper clips, and stamps. You can use #10 envelopes (standard size) which are perfectly acceptable. Or you can use 9"×12" envelopes which keep your resume flat and make it easier for companies to scan.

- **Create a mail merge.** Since you will be sending approximately 50 letters (at least 2 to each of your target companies) in each mailing, you want to be able to print the letters and envelopes quickly and professionally. The Mail Merge tool in Microsoft Word allows you to personalize and print your letters and envelopes using the Excel spreadsheet or Word table you created earlier. You can even include the name of the company in the body of the letter.

  Be sure to proof the letter and each name and address before you begin the Mail Merge.

  ◦ Open Microsoft Word; **if you are using Word 2003**, click on Tools, Letters and Mailings, Mail Merge and follow the steps on the right of the screen to personalize and print your letters.

  ◦ **If you are using Word 2007**, click on Mailings, Start Mail Merge, then choose Step by Step Mail Merge Wizard. Follow the steps at the right of the screen to personalize and print your letters.

- After you print the letters, sign each one and paper clip your resume to the letter.

- Use the mail merge process to print your personalized envelopes.

- Insert the appropriate letter into each envelope, seal, stamp, and mail.

Now that you have built your mailing list and set up your mail merge, you are ready to send another mailing at a later date if need be.

Timing Is Everything
Don't mail cover letters and resumes the week before a holiday. The people to whom you are mailing may be taking some time off.

ACTIVITY 12.3

Practice Mail Merge

Instructions: Create your mailing list using Microsoft Word or Excel in Activity 12.2. Use the mailing list to create a mail merge in Microsoft Word. Follow the steps to create your mail merge to understand how the process works.

Career Fairs

Whenever you have an opportunity to meet a prospective employer in person, do it! Career fairs can be extremely productive. Follow these guidelines to ensure success:

- **Create an action plan.** Before the fair, review the list of employers that will be attending. Review open job listings to identify which employers you will target to meet. Make a list of the employers, contact name (if available), and location at the fair so you have a plan of action. Be open-minded and visit as many companies as possible. Career fairs are an excellent way to learn about companies with which you may not be familiar and jobs that you didn't realize were available. Use Activity 12.4 to prepare for each fair.

ACTIVITY 12.4 My Career Fair Action Plan

Instructions: Before each career fair, review the list of participating companies and complete this action plan.

Date of Career Fair _____

Time of Career Fair _____

Location of Career Fair _____

Target Company Name	Contact Person	How I Bring Value to This Company	Open Jobs	Location of Company Booth at Fair

- **Bring copies of your "advertising."** Print more copies of your cover letter and resume than you expect to give out. Print them on high-quality paper (use white or off-white 24-lb. paper). Carry them in a folder or binder; bent resumes are never professional.

- **Always dress for success.** Wear business attire including shoes, hair, and makeup (if appropriate). Since you will be seeing different kinds of companies, this is not the time to be business casual. Stop in the rest room before you enter the job fair. It's a good time to do a last-minute check and use a breath mint just to be sure.

- **Make a personal contact.** Take the time to introduce yourself to each representative from the companies on your target list. This is an opportunity to introduce your brand so be energetic, professional, and share your value proposition while you are presenting your resume. You are the best advertising for yourself so make each contact work.

- **Ask for a business card.** Follow up with a thank-you note (or e-mail) within 24 hours that refers to your meeting at the career fair. Also, add each person to your mailing list and set a reminder date to follow up in one to week.

Networking

Networking is such an important part of your media mix that Chapter 14 is devoted to how and when to do effective networking.

Follow-up

When you implement an integrated marketing communication plan, you want to follow up quickly and consistently to maximize your return on your investment. Follow-up is one of the most difficult things to do but can be the most effective. When you follow up, you have the opportunity to make a positive impression. In addition, it gives you the chance to identify other people (or the correct people) to whom you should be directing your communication.

Create Your Follow-up Plan

Using the Excel spreadsheet or Word table you created for your mailing list, add four additional columns:

- Date the cover letters and resumes were sent
- Date of follow-up
- Result of follow-up
- Date for second follow-up

Get Organized, Stay Organized

Use the Getting Started Activity in the *Brand You* Toolkit to create your personal job search action plan and timeline.

This spreadsheet or table is an excellent tool to keep track of the dates you agreed to for follow-up. **See the Sample Company Follow-up List at the end of this chapter.**

Here are some guidelines to make your follow-up appropriate and timely:

Follow up to:	When to Follow Up	How to Follow Up	Comments
Job posted on a job board or a Web site	1 week	Phone call to the contact listed in the posting	Many employers do not include a contact name; not all submissions to job postings can include a follow-up.
Direct mail	1 week	Phone call to the person to whom you sent the letter	It's best to call when you are able to talk to the person. Leave a voice mail if necessary, but be sure to follow up again.
			It may not be possible to follow up on every letter sent; choose the top 10–20 for follow-up.
Career fair	1 day	Thank-you note or e-mail to the person you met at the fair	Set a date for follow-up in your thank-you note.
Networking	1 day	Thank-you note or e-mail to the person	Set a date for follow-up in your thank-you note.

ACTIVITY 12.5 Communications Timeline and Action Plan

Instructions: Create your own Communications Timeline and Action Plan by filling in the dates in your Work Plan in the **Brand You** *Toolkit.*

Finding the right job is a big job. Sometimes it may seem like you aren't getting the response you want. Don't get discouraged! You are on the right track and you will find the internship or full-time job you want. Use all the "media" you have available and keep trying!

My Career Journal

Name five resources you will use to identify your target companies.

_____

_____

_____

_____

_____

Name five resources you will use to identify the names, titles, and addresses of people to whom you want to mail your cover letter and resume at your target companies.

_____

_____

_____

_____

_____

List how you will use each of the 7 "media" discussed in Chapter 12 in your own integrated marketing communications plan.

_____

_____

_____

_____

_____

_____

_____

Continue on the next page...

Sample Company Mailing List

	A	B	C	D	E	F	G	H	I	J	K	L	M
1						Sample Company Mailing List							
2	Prefix	First Name	Middle Initial	Last Name	Title	Company Name	Address	Suite #	City	State	Zip Code	Email Address	Phone Number
3	Ms.	Jane	M.	Doe	Vice President of Marketing	Acme International	100 Corporate Drive	101	Philadelphia	PA	19001	jdoe@acme.com	215-123-4567
4	Mr.	Ronald	G.	Hanover	Director of Advertising	Acme International	101 Corporate Drive	101	Philadelphia	PA	19001	rhanover@acme.com	215-123-4579
5	Mr.	Jose		Hernandez	Director of Human Resources	Acme International	101 Corporate Drive	101	Philadelphia	PA	19001	jhernandez@acme.com	215-123-4545
6	Mr.	John	J.	Jones	President	AA Advertising Agency	22 Horizon Circle		Ardmore	PA	19234	jjones@aaagency.com	215-453-1234
7	Ms.	Laura	L.	Lind	Account Director	AA Advertising Agency	23 Horizon Circle		Ardmore	PA	19234	l.lind@aaagency.com	215-453-2489
8	Mr.	Michael	M.	Quinn	Account Director	AA Advertising Agency	24 Horizon Circle		Ardmore	PA	19234	m.quinn@aaagency.com	215-453-2070
9	Ms.	Rene		Lieberman	Human Resources Manager	AA Advertising Agency	25 Horizon Circle		Ardmore	PA	19234	r.lieberman@aaagency.com	215-453-2222
10	Mr.	Steven		Smith	Director of Advertising	Best Company, Inc.	123 First Avenue	2543	Marlton	NJ	84352	ssmith@best.com	809-345-2218
11	Ms.	Allison	K.	Marshal	Vice President of Advertising	Marshall & Associates	45 Main Street		Philadelphia	PA	19191	amarshal@marshall.com	800-222-5555 ext. 100
12	Ms.	Jennifer		Lee	Director of Human Resources	Marshall & Associates	46 Main Street		Philadelphia	PA	19191	jlee@marshall.com	800-222-5555 ext. 109

Sample Company Mailing List with Follow-up

	A	B	C	D	E	F	G	H	I	J	K	L	M	N	O	P	Q
1	Prefix	First Name	Middle Initial	Last Name	Title	Company Name	Address	Suite #	City	State	Zip Code	Email Address	Phone Number	Date Resume Sent	Date of Follow-up	Result of Follow-up	Date for Second Follow-up
2	Ms.	Jane	M.	Doe	Vice President of Marketing	Acme International	100 Corporate Drive	101	Philadelphia	PA	19001	jdoe@acme.com	215-123-4567	3-Feb	12-Feb	call back	1-Mar
3	Mr.	Ronald	G.	Hanover	Director of Advertising	Acme International	101 Corporate Drive	101	Philadelphia	PA	19001	rhanover@acme.com	215-123-4579	3-Feb	12-Feb	no jobs open now	1-Apr
4	Mr.	Jose		Hernandez	Director of Human Resources	Acme International	101 Corporate Drive	101	Philadelphia	PA	19001	jhernandez@acme.com	215-123-4545	3-Feb	12-Feb	no jobs open now	1-Apr
5	Mr.	John	J.	Jones	President	AA Advertising Agency	22 Horizon Circle		Ardmore	PA	19234	jjones@aaagency.com	215-453-1234	3-Feb	13-Feb	no jobs open now	1-Apr
6	Ms.	Laura	L.	Lind	Account Director	AA Advertising Agency	23 Horizon Circle		Ardmore	PA	19234	l.lind@aaagency.com	215-453-2489	3-Feb	13-Feb	no jobs open now	1-Apr
7	Mr.	Michael	M.	Quinn	Account Director	AA Advertising Agency	24 Horizon Circle		Ardmore	PA	19234	m.quinn@aaagency.com	215-453-2070	3-Feb	13-Feb	interview Feb 22	
8	Ms.	Rene		Lieberman	Human Resources Manager	AA Advertising Agency	25 Horizon Circle		Ardmore	PA	19234	r.lieberman@aaagency.com	215-453-2222	3-Feb	15-Feb	call back	5-Mar
9	Mr.	Steven		Smith	Director of Advertising	Best Company, Inc.	123 First Avenue	2543	Marlton	NJ	84352	ssmith@best.com	809-345-2218	3-Feb	15-Feb	call back	5-Mar
10	Ms.	Allison	K.	Marshal	Vice President of Advertising	Marshall & Associates	45 Main Street		Philadelphia	PA	19191	amarshal@marshall.com	800-222-5555 ext. 100	3-Feb	15-Feb	interview Feb 22	
11	Ms.	Jennifer		Lee	Director of Human Resources	Marshall & Associates	46 Main Street		Philadelphia	PA	19191	jlee@marshall.com	800-222-5555 ext. 109	3-Feb	15-Feb	call back	5-Mar

Notes to **Myself**

13

Advertising Your Brand:
Crafting Your Resumé and Cover Letter

Resumés and cover letters serve the same function as advertising—they educate potential employers about a product (you) and what it does. A resumé emphasizes your features (your skills, knowledge, and experience) and your benefits. Most television ads last 30 seconds; that's about how long you have to grab your reader's attention. Therefore, your cover letter and resumé should generate a desire to learn more about you—they should create impact and generate interest.

Have you ever wondered how recruiters evaluate resumés? If you're applying for an advertised position, your resumé is probably somewhere in a crowded e-mail inbox. Most recruiters don't take the time to read each one. Instead, they glance over each cover letter and maybe the resumé for less than 30 seconds and determine if they will delete or keep each one. The cover letters and resumés that are automatically deleted are those with typos, misspellings, or those that are bizarre. Then the recruiter scans the cover letters and resumés that are left. You must capture his attention quickly, so he will slow down and read about your accomplishments. Regardless of how many people have applied for the position, generally recruiters select a maximum of 10 people to interview for each job opening.

Your cover letter and resumé are critical marketing tools—they are your communication of the proof regarding your skills, educational background, and accomplishments. They must say, "I can add value to your organization." Your cover letter and resumé by themselves won't land a job—their purpose is to get you invited for an interview.

Objectives

1. How do I write an effective resumé?
2. How can I get my resumé noticed by employers?
3. How do I write a cover letter that grabs attention?

In this chapter, we'll examine the elements needed for a dynamic cover letter and resumé that get noticed. While cover letters and resumés are a critical aspect of your ad campaign, they don't have to be agonizing to write. Step by step, you'll learn how to organize your information, write clear, concise descriptions, and select the format that's best for you.

The approach to cover letter and resumé writing that you'll learn here will differentiate you from other job hunters. You'll learn how to focus on the needs of the employers you've targeted, and describe your experience in terms that are relevant to those needs. Not only will your cover letter and resumé pass the first test and avoid being deleted, it will also present your abilities in ways that relate to the skills the employer is seeking. By following this approach, you can expect invitations to come in for an interview.

Joe
Chernov's Brand

You met Joe in **Chapter 13** *of* Marketing: Real People, Real Choices. *He's director of public relations for BzzAgent, Inc., a word-of-mouth marketing and media firm based in Boston.*

▼ **Q** & **A** with Joe Chernov

Key word:
Candid.

Distinctive competency:
An ability to understand what others are *really* saying.

My brand image:
Unconventional. An effective brand is holistic: all elements need to be in synch for it to work. In my particular case, the elements include peculiar word choice, idiosyncratic attire, unexpected candor, and lots and lots of tattoos.

One value I create for the company:
A willingness to scrap conventional wisdom in favor of unorthodox solutions to common problems.

Joe's Advice
To prepare for the workplace:
Be humble. Please. Realize that your degree entitles you only to an opportunity to prove you can apply what you have learned. Congratulations. You have the rare luxury of a clean slate.

A job-hunting strategy I would definitely use:
I would consider my first job as an investment in myself. I would imagine where I wanted to be professionally in 10 years, and pursue all positions that could put me on that track—even if it meant sacrificing income or social status for the first few years. I would view it as paid continuing education.

How a student can overcome lack of experience:
Have faith in man's inherent desire to impart knowledge. There is nothing wrong with applying for an entry-level position (or internship) and telling the interviewer that you want this position for the opportunity to learn from him or her. This technique will not only appeal to the individual's professional vanity, but it will also separate you from the hordes of "entitled" job seekers.

The benefit of a personal brand:
Brands, like careers, are built over time. Just as it is inconceivable for a product to establish a true brand presence overnight, so too is it unrealistic for a young professional to order up a personal brand. But once earned, a personal brand is an invaluable asset when it comes to navigating internal politics, earning customer/client confidence, and networking for new positions.

The NAB Process

The secret to writing dynamic resumés and cover letters is using the NAB (Need, Action, Benefit) process. **Employers want proof that you have the skills you say you do.** This is critical to developing your own personal brand. *Employers believe that past performance predicts future performance.* So, if you can describe the skills and the results you have achieved, you will convince employers that you'll use them in the future. Once you've written the Action and Benefit statements, you have most of the information you need to construct a compelling resumé.

With the NAB process you can demonstrate that you've actually used the skills the employer is seeking. You'll notice in our examples that past jobs are not the only reference you can use. For instance, you can also describe skills you've acquired while completing class assignments, participating in campus activities, and completing internships.

Need. What does the employer need or want? Identify an employer's needs and the problems you can solve. Look at job descriptions, talk to employers, read trade journals, and visit Web sites.

Action. How have you demonstrated each skill? Write down a time when you used each skill or knowledge. Include who, what, where, and why.

Benefit. What was the result of your action? Describe the results you achieved—the benefit of your skills in the situation. Use numbers, dollars, and percentages whenever you can.

Student Profile—Chris

Chris found a job description for the type of position she is seeking—a marketing assistant. She highlighted the skills, knowledge, and characteristics that the employer wanted. These are the employer's needs.

Marketing Assistant

We're Optibiz Corporation, a leading supplier of optics, photonics instruments and components, optomechanical components, positioning equipment, and vibration control. We are currently seeking a detail-oriented and highly motivated marketing assistant. Selected candidate will assist in the development and implementation of promotional marketing activities in our vibration control group. This will include: forecasting marketing trends of new/existing products; developing catalogs, brochures, and other collateral material; tracking and reporting advertising/collateral budget expenditures; implementing trade show efforts; and supporting product management processes. Requires a bachelor's degree in marketing or 3+ years applicable marketing experience. Knowledge of MS Excel is essential. We offer an excellent compensation and benefits package, a leading-edge work environment, and opportunities for professional growth. We invite qualified candidates to send or fax a resumé to. . . .

Next, Chris completed a NAB worksheet. She listed the needs she had highlighted in the job description. Then she added some characteristics she knew from her research were important to hiring managers in marketing departments. After completing this activity, Chris realized she had more experience related to marketing than she thought she had. She was much more confident about her chances to land the kind of job she wanted. You'll be happily surprised too!

Chris' NAB Worksheet

Need **What does the employer need? (Skills, experience, knowledge)**	Action **How have you demonstrated each skill or knowledge?**	Benefit **What was the result?**
Detail-oriented	Accounting clerk Developed reports and charts using Excel	Accurately maintained accounts receivable; reduced delinquent accounts by 20 percent
Highly motivated	Worked while maintaining high grade point average	3.8 GPA
Forecast market trends	Marketing class—wrote paper forecasting market trends in publishing	Learned how to research and forecast trends
Develop brochure	Fundraiser	Helped write fund-raising flyer, raised $1,800 for local charity
Track budget	Treasurer, American Marketing Student Association. Tracked income and expenses using Excel	Kept accurate records of membership dues and expenses
Trade show	Canvassed local residents for reelection campaign	Learned to be comfortable informing and persuading people
Excel	Designed new format for reporting accounts receivable	Streamlined reporting and facilitated collections
Develop collateral materials	Term papers	Excellent comments on PowerPoint visuals; writing skills
Communication skills	Speech class, club treasurer	Received an "A" in speech class; treasurer's reports helped us set goals
Teamwork	Study group	Kept group on track by facilitating discussions—received an "A" on project
Creative	Voter registration Web site	Posted articles geared to young people; increased voter registrations by 20 percent

Use NAB to Communicate Your Value

Instructions: Complete the worksheet below using a job description and other information about skills, knowledge, and characteristics that employers in your field seek in job candidates. Write these in the "Need" column. Use your experiences in school, work, internships, or volunteer activities to fill in the "Action" column. Describe the benefits of the results you achieved in the last column, using numbers or percentages whenever possible.

Need **What does the employer need?** **(Skills, experience, knowledge)**	Action **How have you demonstrated** **each skill or knowledge?**	Benefit **What was the result?**

Writing a Dynamic Resumé

Writing a resumé can seem like a daunting task, but if you follow the steps outlined below, you'll find it manageable—not nearly as intimidating as filling a blue book or writing a research paper!

Get Organized

Review your NAB worksheet. Be sure you've included all relevant experiences such as jobs, internships, scholarships and honors, extracurricular activities, class projects, volunteer activities, and coursework. Gather addresses, phone numbers, and dates for each experience.

Never lie or exaggerate on your resumé. Employers can verify all the information you provide. They can confirm your education, previous employment, association memberships, and more. Stretching the truth will come back to haunt you. Most people are tempted to exaggerate because they lack confidence in their abilities or their experience. Remember that some employers prefer new college grads—your task is to find out which ones. Boost your chances by applying for jobs for which you are a good fit and by tailoring your message to their needs.

Decide on the Type of Resumé

There are two general resumé types: chronological and functional. **For most people, a chronological resumé that lists your work experience beginning with your most recent position is the best choice.** For one thing, it is the style with which people are most familiar. If you are applying to large, traditional companies this is the style to choose.

On the other hand, if you are changing careers, or have gaps in your education/work history, a functional resumé may be best. This style resumé highlights specific skills rather than your chronological work experience. Group your skills into categories, regardless of whether you learned them in school or acquired them on the job. For example, a person majoring in marketing might select these categories: market research, writing, editing, and computer skills. You still include your work history, but you list the jobs you have held at the bottom with the dates of employment on the right side of the page, where they are less obvious.

Build the Framework

Identifying Information

The top of your resumé should include your full name, both your campus address and your home address, phone number(s), and e-mail address. Your name should be the most prominent item on your resumé. Use bold, 14- to 16-point type.

Headings

Organize the content of your resumé by using headings. This makes it easier for the reader to find the information for which they are looking. Following are headings for you to consider.

Resumé Essentials

- Identifying information
- Job objective or skills summary
- Education
- Work experience
- Key words
- Correct spelling and grammar

Appeal to Your Target
Most people gear their resume toward getting another job just like their last one. The secret to advancing your career is to focus on the needs of your *next* employer.

Skills Summary, Profile, Summary of Qualifications, or Career Objective.   Start your resumé with one of these headings. The advantage of a skills summary, profile, or summary of qualifications is that you can highlight your accomplishments and characteristics to grab interest immediately. Refer back to your value proposition in Chapter 9 to write your summary or profile. Include one or two sentences, followed by bullets that highlight your skills and personal characteristics. An objective shows a potential employer that you know what path you want to pursue.

Sample Skills Summary or Profile: Use bulleted statements such as the following:

- Ability to conduct market research and predict consumer trends
- Creative writer skilled in designing content that appeals to audience
- Tuned in to the young-adult demographic

Sample Summary of Qualifications: Use bulleted statements such as the following:

- Personable and persuasive; able to build instant rapport
- Well organized and self-motivated
- Creative, energetic, positive attitude

Sample Objective: Seeking a public relations position requiring writing and interpersonal skills.

Education.   For new grads, education is often the most relevant qualification for the position. If this is true for you, it should be described right after your summary or objective. List the school(s) you've attended and the degree you are earning. **If your GPA is 3.5 or higher, include it. If it is lower than 3.5, don't include it. Your GPA is not a requirement.** Don't list high school unless you took some courses that are particularly relevant.

Honors and Scholarships: List honors, scholarships, or honor society membership.

Work History.   You can use any one of a variety of headings to describe your work history. Choices include: Work History, Employment History, Professional Experience, or Work Experience. You should include internship experience in your work history.

Additional Headings.   Depending on your background, you may want to include additional headings, such as Related Projects.

Skills: Include software and other skills. For example, Proficient in Microsoft Word, Excel, PowerPoint and Outlook.

Additional Qualifications: List accomplishments in extracurricular activities or abilities such as fluency in another language.

Memberships: List professional or school organizations to which you belong.

Describe Your Career History

This is the most important section of your resumé. Use the NAB process so that your resumé focuses on the needs of the employer. Most people gear their resumé toward getting another job just like their last one. Now that you've earned your degree, you no doubt want to change careers—or at least your level of responsibility. That's why you want to emphasize your accomplishments that relate to what your *next* employer wants—not what your last one wanted.

Another advantage of using the NAB process is that it makes it easy to customize your resumé to specific employers. Think of your action and benefit statements as a database of information about your accomplishments. After researching an employer's needs (by referring to the job description, Web site, and insider information) you can change or rearrange your accomplishment statements so that the ones most important to this employer are at the top of each section.

- List three to five accomplishments for each employment or internship experience. If you have had an internship or other relevant work experience, be sure to include at least 4–5 bullet points about your accomplishments. Use fewer bullet points (and less space) for summer jobs. Make important things important by allocating the most space to the most important things such as internships and related work experience.
- Describe results, quantifying as often as possible. For example, "Developed new marketing strategy, increasing market share by 10 percent."
- Use bulleted statements starting with an **action verb**. See the list of verbs later in this chapter to help you.
- Do not use phrases found in job descriptions such as, "Responsible for. . . ." Instead, describe what you did and the results you achieved, using action verbs.
- Choose one tense, either past or present, and use it throughout your resumé.

Format and Edit

Looks Count

- Choose a font that's easy to read, such as Times, Arial, Helvetica, or Palatino. Don't use different fonts within your resumé, although it is fine to use bold for headings or emphasis within the font you've selected.
- The easiest way to achieve formatting consistency is to **use a two-column table**. Use a narrow first column for your headings and dates; use a larger column for the descriptions of your accomplishments. When you're done, click the Format menu and delete the borders.
- Your margins should be between 1/2" and 1".
- Use lots of white space so that your resumé is easy to read. If you are just graduating or out of school for only a few years, your resumé should not exceed one page. Edit your text if your resumé appears cramped.
- Highlight job titles, employers, and other resumé categories such as education with bold type. Avoid using all capital letters, underlining, or

Tips for a Scannable Resumé

With the latest in technology, organizations, particularly in the government sector, are turning to the electronic process of scanning. It will search for degrees, titles, organizations, and other information specific to a particular opening.

- Include key words—nouns that are listed in the job description. Match the words exactly. Computers can't evaluate; they can only match.
- Use standard typefaces and fonts between 12 and 14 points in size.
- Avoid italics, underlines, and shadows.
- Shoot for simplicity.
- Avoid vertical and horizontal lines, graphics, and boxes.

Video Resumés

A video resumé can be a novel approach to job searching, but do one only if you are extremely comfortable in front of the camera. Follow the same guidelines as a traditional resumé. And, be sure your resumé is also available as a Word document since less than 25 percent of companies currently use video resumés. Here are five tips for a successful video resumé:

- Keep it professional and businesslike.
- Keep it short (one to three minutes).
- Practice, practice, practice.
- Get feedback from mentors.
- Post to job sites such as **www.careerbuilder.com**, **www.jobster.com**, **www. linkedin.com** and your professional Web site.

italics. Be consistent—use the same style for each corresponding heading (e.g., Objective, Employment).

- **Be absolutely certain there are no typos or misspellings.** Ask someone (such as a professor, your parents, or working professional) to proof your resumé for you.
- Don't use a template—your resumé, like you, should be unique.
- Use a laser printer and print your resumé on white or neutral-colored 24-lb. bond paper.

Action Verb List

Accomplish	Design	Install	Publicize
Achieve	Detail	Institute	Publish
Adapt	Determine	Instruct	Recommend
Administer	Develop	Integrate	Reconcile
Advertise	Devise	Interpret	Recruit
Advise	Direct	Interview	Rectify
Affect	Distribute	Invent	Redesign
Analyze	Draft	Investigate	Relate
Anticipate	Edit	Lead	Renew
Apply	Educate	Maintain	Report
Approach	Employ	Manage	Represent
Approve	Encourage	Manipulate	Research
Arrange	Enlarge	Market	Reshape
Assemble	Enlist	Mediate	Resolve
Assess	Establish	Merchandise	Review
Assign	Estimate	Moderate	Revise
Assist	Evaluate	Modify	Scan
Budget	Examine	Monitor	Schedule
Build	Exchange	Motivate	Screen
Calculate	Execute	Negotiate	Secure
Catalog	Expand	Obtain	Select
Chair	Expedite	Operate	Serve
Clarify	Facilitate	Organize	Staff
Coach	Familiarize	Originate	Standardize
Collaborate	Forecast	Participate	Stimulate
Compare	Formulate	Perceive	Strengthen
Conceive	Generate	Perform	Suggest
Conceptualize	Govern	Persuade	Summarize
Conduct	Guide	Plan	Supervise
Construct	Handle	Prepare	Survey
Consult	Hire	Present	Systematize
Contract	Identify	Preside	Teach
Contribute	Implement	Problem solve	Team build
Control	Improve	Process	Train
Coordinate	Increase	Produce	Update
Counsel	Index	Program	Utilize
Create	Influence	Project	Verify
Decide	Inform	Promote	Write
Define	Initiate	Prompt	
Delegate	Innovate	Propose	
Demonstrate	Inspect	Provide	

Sample Chronological Resumé

Carlos Miranda
120 Stapley Street
San Francisco, California 94105
(415) 352-6834; cmiranda@hotmail.com

Career Objective To obtain Marketing Assistant position involving market research and analysis

Education Bachelor of Science in Business Administration, emphasis in Marketing Golden Gate University, San Francisco, CA

> Carlos emphasizes his education and course work related to his career objective.

Work Experience
3/2003–Present

Gap, Inc., San Francisco, CA Assistant Store Manager

- Conducted research and analysis to identify new customers
- Designed new marketing strategies that increased store traffic by 25 percent
- Developed monthly plans to increase sales, resulting in increased profits
- Calculated daily sales, and wrote accurate sales reports

> In his descriptions, Carlos tells what he did and the results he achieved.

Fall 2006

American Heart Association, San Francisco, CA Intern

- Created fund-raiser publicity, raising $1,800
- Coordinated targeted marketing plan, resulting in new corporate sponsors
- Assisted in research and prepared data and figures for reports to Board of Directors

3/2001–3/2003

Crate and Barrel, San Francisco, CA Accounting Clerk

- Maintained accounts receivable, reducing delinquent accounts by 20 percent
- Improved tracking of accounts receivable by creating reports using Excel software
- Implemented new accounting procedure, increasing accounting process efficiency

Computer Skills Microsoft Word, Excel, PowerPoint, Outlook

Honors and Activities National Honor Society
Speech Club Treasurer
Peer Tutor in Accounting Principles, 2003–2004
Program Chair, Marketing Club

Sample Functional Resumé

Jennifer DiCarlo

123 Main Street Tempe, AZ 85245 (602) 345-6789

Profile	• Civil engineer knowledgeable in environmental issues • Results-oriented professional who achieves project goals • Proficient in a wide variety of computer software programs • Experienced team leader for engineering projects
Education	B.S. in Engineering, Civil and Environmental Engineering Arizona State University, Tempe, AZ GPA 3.6; Dean's List three semesters while working part-time.
Skills	Software—AUTO CAD, GS-USA, MS Word, Excel, PowerPoint, FileMaker Pro, Aldus PageMaker Languages—HTML and BASIC

> **Jennifer highlights her computer skills.**

> **She describes engineering projects she completed in college.**

Projects

Steel Structures—Designed various angles, channels, columns, and frames under given design criteria.

Structural Analysis—Designed a truss-and-frame bridge to span 18-foot gulch supporting a load of 5,000 lb/ft. Used GS-USA software for final checks.

Senior Design Project—"College Avenue Traffic Calming and Pedestrian Bridge Improvement Plan" to solve parking congestion, increase safety, improve aesthetics, and reduce volume and speed on actual road in Tempe. Plan included modifications to pedestrian bridge to meet ADA specifications. Completed cost estimates, proposal, and AutoCAD drawings.

Surveying—Performed a building layout, including elevations, contours, location of trees, lines, and sidewalks, submitting project as blueprint with title block and legal description.

Highway—Designed a two-lane highway section with an intersection. Design included critical and horizontal curves, drainage culverts, and cut/fill calculations.

> **Because her work experience isn't very relevant, she puts it at the end. Notice the location of her employment dates.**

Work Experience

Industrial Associates Program, Arizona State University, Tempe, AZ Administrative Assistant 2/2004 to present
• Created and updated on-line home page describing program goals and special events.
• Designed visually attractive PowerPoint presentations for papers and conferences.
• Assisted in collection, tabulation, and presentation of data.

Sample Internship Resumé

Christine Matthews

813 E. Wetmore Place   (520) 345-7888
Tucson, AZ 85710   CMatthews23@msn.com

Objective	Seeking internship in market research
Skills Summary	• Easily establish rapport with people from all walks of life • Research client demographics to assist in developing marketing campaign • Analyze data to find salient points and trend information • Completed coursework in marketing and market research • Creative writing style, able to engage audience • Skilled in HTML, Word, and Excel
Education	University of Arizona, Tucson, Arizona Business major with emphasis in marketing. Degree expected in June, 2008 Selected as member of Blue Key National Honorary Society Work full-time while maintaining a 3.8 GPA
Internship	Account Services Intern, **The Householder Group**, Tucson, Arizona Summer 2005 • Researched client demographics for this retail seafood consultancy • Updated Web site including content and photography for 200 new products per month, increasing site visitors by 45% • Created daily Web site report for senior management using Coremetrics Web analytics tool • Managed over 500 paid search keywords which accounted for over 30% of Web site sales, decreased cost per click by 4% • Assisted in writing marketing brochures and other collateral used at trade shows
Employment	Accounting Clerk, **Anthropologie**, Tucson, AZ Sept. 2004–present • Accurately maintain income and debit accounts • Develop monthly and quarterly income reports using Excel Server, **Ten Restaurant**, Tucson, AZ Sept. 2003–June 2004 • Took orders and served customers • Used Aloha computer system
Activities	• As a volunteer, wrote a fund-raising brochure for Breast Cancer Foundation of Arizona; campus event raised $1,800 for the charity • Treasurer, American Marketing Student Association Student • Canvassed neighborhoods to promote reelection of a political candidate

> Chris includes her expected graduation date and degree.

> Chris lists other internship first to highlight her most relevant experience.

Writing a Powerful Cover Letter

Don't underestimate the power of your cover letter!

Your cover letter can be your most important advertising. Although a potential employer is most interested in your resumé, your cover letter positions your brand and gets your resumé read. Many resumés are never even seen because of bad cover letters. Take the time to write a compelling cover letter.

Just like there are different styles of resumés, there are two styles of cover letters—narrative style or the narrative style with bullet points. Both use the same basic elements described below.

The narrative style is a traditional business letter and is written in full sentences throughout. This style gives you an opportunity to showcase your writing skills. Jennifer DiCarlo's cover letter (Figure 13.2) is an example of narrative style.

The narrative style with bullet points incorporates bullet points in the second paragraph to highlight the key benefits of your brand. Carlos Miranda's cover letter (Figure 13.1) is an example of this style. The advantage of the narrative style with bullet points is that it makes it easier for the reader to visually scan rather than read the entire letter. When an employer scans a good cover letter, he or she usually reads it completely, then reads the resumé. And, the narrative style with bullet points can be easier to write.

Paragraph One—The Introduction

See More

There are more sample cover letters and resumés in the *Brand You* Toolkit.

The introduction provides your chance to grab readers and entice them to read on. Most cover letters are very boring reading. Find something interesting to say, create visibility and impact, and your letter will leap out from the stack recruiters are reviewing. **Talk about the position you are seeking, how you learned about the position, and whatever it is that interests you most about the position.**

Carlos Miranda wrote the cover letter in Figure 13.1 to reply to a specific ad in the newspaper. Note how he researched the company on the Internet to find a good way to open his letter and gain the reader's attention. A colleague referred Jennifer DiCarlo to Ms. Owens, so she gets the reader's attention by mentioning the mutual contact in the first paragraph (see Figure 13.2).

Paragraph Two—The Body of the Letter

Don't Forget Your Keywords

It's important that you use key words in your resumé as well as your cover letter so employers can scan (by computer and visually) to see exactly what your brand represents.

Use the body of the letter to emphasize your experience and its relevancy to the specific position. Describe examples to show that you have the qualifications the employer is seeking. Cite accomplishments as they relate to the desired characteristics. List particular skills and academic achievements that

Figure 13.1 Carlos Miranda's cover letter—narrative style with bullet points

> **Carlos Miranda**
> **120 Stapley Street**
> **San Francisco, CA 94105**
>
> May 15, 2008
>
> Ms. Diane Thomson
> Director of Marketing
> Optiflex Corporation
> 4333 West 56th Street
> San Francisco, CA 94000
>
> Dear Ms. Thomson,
>
> The introduction of the FXY-09 must be creating exciting opportunities within the Marketing Department. After exploring the Optiflex Web site, it is apparent that Optiflex is marketing specifically to consumers for the first time. You will require someone to develop marketing strategies that achieve your goals and are delivered on time and on budget. I would like to be a part of this effort.
>
> Recently, I earned my Bachelor of Science degree in Business Administration with an emphasis in Marketing from Golden Gate University. My degree along with my work experience in marketing, sales and accounting makes me uniquely qualified for a position in the Marketing Department. Some highlights of my achievements are the following:
>
> - **Marketing Experience**. As an intern at the American Heart Association, I worked with a team to create the advertising materials for a successful direct marketing campaign that raised $1,800. I conducted the research on the local market and recommended the targets for the campaign.
>
> - **Sales Experience**. I understand what it takes to make sales happen at the store level. In my role as Assistant Store Manager at Gap, I conducted research and analysis to identify new customers and designed new marketing strategies that increased store traffic by 25 percent.
>
> - **Leadership Skills**. I have demonstrated responsibility, accountability, and leadership in my roles as Speech Club Treasurer and Program Chair of the Marketing Club during my academic career.
>
> - **Academic Achievement**. My grades and activities earned me membership in the National Honor Society during my junior year.
>
> I'd like the opportunity to show you samples of my work and discuss in more detail how my experience and skills are a good fit for the Optiflex Corporation. I will call you during the week of May 19 to set up a convenient time to meet. I can be reached at (415)352-6834 or cmiranda@hotmail.com. Thank you for your consideration. I look forward to speaking with you.
>
> Sincerely,
>
>
> Carlos Miranda
>
> Attachment

demonstrate you are a good match for the job. Use your NAB activity to determine the two to four key points you want to make.

Note the difference in style between Jennifer's cover letter (Figure 13.2), which uses the narrative style and Carlos's cover letter, which uses the narrative style with bullet points (Figure 13.1).

Figure 13.2 Jennifer DiCarlo's cover letter—narrative style

JENNIFER DICARLO

August 31, 2008

Ms. Jessica Owens
Director of Engineering
Bradford and Associates
4557 West London Road
Boston, MA 02115

Dear Ms. Owens,

Brad Peterman suggested that I contact you regarding an entry-level engineering position. I worked with Brad on my Senior Design Project. He was the primary engineer for the City of Tempe assigned to this traffic improvement project. He felt there could be a good match between my skills and your firm. I am very interested in working for a firm with such a strong history of supporting women civil engineers.

I recently graduated from Arizona State University with a Bachelor of Science degree in Civil and Environmental Engineering. I have experience working on projects involving steel structures, highway design, and geotechnical foundations. My computer skills are excellent. I am familiar with most engineering software. People tell me I have a real aptitude to pick up technical computer programs quickly.

I grew up on the East Coast and would be very interested in relocating to the Boston area. I will call you next week to set up an appointment to discuss my qualifications in further detail. I am planning on being in the Boston area the second week of September. Thanks for your time and consideration.

Sincerely,

Jennifer DiCarlo

Attachment

12345 MAIN STREET · TEMPE, ARIZONA 12345 · (602) 456-7890
e-mail jenn@greatenvironments.com

Make a Portfolio

Put samples of your work into a binder, including major projects from your internship or classes, volunteer activities, presentations, and writing samples or articles you have written. Close your cover letter with a request to show samples of your work to the prospective employer. It's the perfect call to action and reason for you to follow-up.

In his cover letter, Carlos discusses his degree and experience as it relates to the marketing position he wants. He describes how his internship gave him the opportunity to put his education to work and achieve real results.

Paragraph Three—The Closing

End your cover letter with an active strategy to get the interview. Offer to show samples of your work and tell the reader that you will call to set up a convenient time to meet and discuss your qualifications further. Thank the reader for his or her time and consideration. Remember to follow up with a phone call.

Cover Letter Format

While there is some flexibility in choosing your cover letter format, there are some elements that are required. See Figure 13.3—Anatomy of a Cover Letter.

Figure 13.3 Anatomy of a Cover Letter

Jonathan Vitale ①
541 North Elm Street
Dayton, OH 12345

②
April 21, 2008

Mr. Michael Woods
Account Director
③ Lane Interactive Advertising
4040 Century Boulevard; Suite 1501
Boston, MA 03456

④ Dear Mr. Woods,

⑤ Congratulations on landing the Dominos Pizza account. I'm sure it's an exciting time at the agency. If you are looking for a motivated individual with a passion for the internet on your team, I am that person.

⑥ I am currently a junior at Brookstone College pursuing a major in Marketing with a focus on Interactive Marketing. I'd like to bring my energy and internet savvy to Lane Interactive Advertising for a summer internship position on one of your client service teams. Some highlights of my background include

⑦
- **Leadership Experience** – As the Student Chairperson of the Event Committee for the Saint Katherine's Youth Group, I have organized over 8 fund-raising events. As a result of the increased fund-raising, our group was able to provide financial assistance and personal support to over 300 local families in need.

- **Professional Trade Group Involvement** – I have gained exposure to the interactive advertising industry as a member of the local chapter of the American Marketing Association and a student member of the Boston Advertising Club.

- **Passion for the Internet** – I thrive on the fact that the internet is continuously evolving and providing new and untapped opportunities for brands. I want to play a role in building brands on-line. As an experienced Internet and technology user, I have the experience and insight to understand how current interactive marketing works and ideas as to how it might work even better.

⑧ With Dominos as a new client, you need only the best people to support the brand. I am focused and willing to work hard in order to learn the business. I would like the opportunity to show you some examples of my work. I can be reached at 615-333-5555 or via e-mail at jvitale@brookstonecollege.edu. I will touch base next week to see which day will be most convenient for you. I look forward to discussing your new challenges.

⑨ Sincerely,

⑩
Jonathan Vitale

⑪ Attachment

1. **Your name and return address.** Should be bold face and in a type size at least one size larger than the body of the letter. *Leave at least one line between your return address and the date.*
2. **Date.** Use month, date, year; spell out month. *Leave one line between the date and the inside address.*
3. **Inside Address.** The name, title, company and address (including suite number if applicable) of the person to whom you are sending the letter. Always use Mr. or Ms. before the first name. Use the person's formal first name and middle initial, if available. *Leave one line between the inside address and the greeting.*
4. **Greeting.** Always use Mr. or Ms. with the last name if you do not know the person on a first name basis. The greeting should be followed by a comma or a colon (Dear Ms. Williams,). If a name is not included in a job posting, the greeting should be, Dear Sir or Madam, or Dear Employer. *Leave one line between the greeting and the first paragraph.*
5. **First paragraph or lead-in line.** This is where you create interest or make a statement about the company. This paragraph may also include your introduction. *Leave one line between first paragraph and second paragraph.*
6. **Second paragraph.** This is where you establish how you can bring value to the company. This should also include your introduction and the position in which you have interest if you didn't include this in the first paragraph/lead-in line.
7. **Bullet points.** Here is where you make your NAB come alive and make it easy for the reader to see what you have to offer to the company at a glance. Use bold face to highlight the key lead-in words. *Leave one line between bullet points.*
8. **Closing paragraph.** This is your call to action; offer to show samples of your work if you have them. Also state when you will follow-up. Give your contact information for easy follow-up. *Leave one line between the last paragraph of the letter and the closing.*
9. **Closing.** "Sincerely" is the standard professional closing. The closing always includes a comma. *Leave four lines between the closing and your name.*
10. **Signature.** Your name. You sign the letter in the space between "Sincerely," and your name. *Leave one line after your name.*
11. **Attachment designation.** Type the word "Attachment" to signify that there is an attachment to the letter (this is comparable to the paperclip that appears on e-mail messages that have an attachment).

TIP: If you are sending a cover letter and resumé via direct mail, paperclip your resumé to your cover letter to prevent them from being separated.

Obtaining References

Thank Your References

Sample thank-you notes are included in the *Brand You* Toolkit.

References are a very misunderstood and misused tool in the job-search process. It's good to have letters of recommendation to demonstrate your experience during an interview. However, employers also want to talk to references personally.

Most employers will request professional references. These are people who can attest to your professional skills—employers, co-workers, professors, and colleagues. Many employers also ask for personal references—people who have known you personally, preferably for five years or more, and can vouch for your character. It's best to select professionally employed people to use as personal references. Don't use your relatives; everyone expects your mother to give you a glowing report.

Lukewarm references can be as damaging as negative ones. Be sure that yours are excellent by asking people if they feel comfortable allowing you to use them as a reference.

Here are the best practices to secure references:

- Call each person you want to use as a reference shortly before you begin your job or internship search. You should have at least three professional references.
- Provide each person on your reference list with a copy of your resumé so he or she can be fluent with the details of your background.
- Explain to each person on your reference list the types of positions for which you are applying.
- Send a hand-written thank-you note to each person on your reference list thanking him or her for speaking on your behalf.
- Keep each person up-to-date on your job search. These people are interested in your career progress and it's a good reason to touch base even if you have no news.
- Let each person on your reference list know when you have accepted a position.

Figure 13.4 References for Carlos Miranda

References for Carlos Miranda

Ms. Megan Stipple
Director of Marketing
American Heart Association
5353 Huron Street
San Francisco, CA 94949
(949)233-2323
m.stipple@aha.org
Relationship: Megan Stipple was my immediate supervisor at American Heart Association.

Dr. Dane Wyant
Professor
Golden Gate University
San Francisco, CA 94900
(415)444-4444
d.wyant@goldengate.edu
Relationship: Dr. Wyant was my faculty advisor and professor for marketing classes.

Ms. Kalina Li
Store Manager
Gap
9495 Mall Drive
San Francisco, CA 94949
(949)088-0000
kli@gap.com
Relationship: Kalina Li was my manager at Gap.

My Career Journal

After completing NAB, what are the two actions you've taken that you enjoyed most?

_____
_____
_____
_____
_____
_____

List 10 action verbs you could use on a resumé from your last job, internship, or volunteer experience.

_____
_____
_____
_____
_____
_____

List three professional references you could use now and why you would want to.

_____
_____
_____
_____
_____
_____

List three personal references you could use now and why you would want to.

_____
_____
_____
_____
_____
_____

Notes to **Myself**

14
Personal Selling:
How Networking Can Help You Achieve Your Goals

Objectives

1. How can I build my personal network?

2. How can I connect with the hidden job market?

3. How can networking increase my chances for success?

Whether you are launching your professional career, seeking an internship, or looking for part-time work, as a job hunter you face the same challenge as a product marketer. How can you stand out among the many eager applicants who bombard employers? Successful job hunters know they have to capture the attention of employers and relate to their needs.

Employers are looking for a person with a particular set of skills and knowledge. In addition, they hope the person will fit in with other employees and collaborate with the team. Your fundamental task as a job hunter is to communicate compelling reasons to hire you. **The best way to do this is to tailor your message to your customer and show them that you have the skills and knowledge they seek.**

Another way to connect with employers is to find ways to communicate with them directly. Marketers know that personal selling can be tremendously effective, especially for big ticket items (and from the employer's perspective, you *are* a big ticket item!). **You can take an active role in your job search, linking with people you know and people you'll meet to help connect with the person who can hire you.**

In this chapter, we will look at all your communications with prospective employers and discuss how to deliver a consistent, compelling message that appeals to your target market. We'll also discuss strategies for connecting directly to employers through networking.

The Hidden Job Market

As you may have heard, tapping into the hidden job market is the best way to find work. The *hidden job market* refers to all of the work that needs doing and hasn't yet been advertised. If you wonder whether this job market exists, or whether it's worth pursuing, consider the following scenario. For a moment, put yourself in the shoes of a manager who just received a resignation from a valued employee. What would you do if you were that manager? Like other managers, you'd probably feel more comfortable hiring someone who has been recommended than an unknown person who looks good on a resumé. First, you might ask employees in your department if they know someone who could do the work. If this doesn't lead to a referral, you'd ask other managers, and colleagues in your professional network. As a last resort, you'd call the human resources department and advertise the position. Why? You dread the typical hiring scenario: sorting through the onslaught of resumés, conducting rounds of interviews, and checking references.

Networking is the way you can connect with the hidden job market— becoming the candidate who is recommended before the job is advertised. The odds of finding a job through networking are much greater than responding to the same ads as everyone else. **Research consistently shows that 80 percent of jobs are filled through networking.** Yet, most people spend their job search time and energy scanning Web sites and newspaper ads. Instead, you should spend a significant effort constantly identifying people in your network.

How Networking Can Help

We've already discussed talking to professionals in your field as the best way to research career possibilities. Of course, when you did that, you were networking. If you haven't connected with professionals yet, here's another nudge for you to try it. If you've been reading the advice of the Real People we interviewed, you'll notice that nearly all of them talk about having passion for the work you're seeking. It's hard to have passion if you don't know much about something. Hearing people talk about their work, why they like it and the satisfaction they feel, brings it to life. Through them, you'll know whether the work aligns with your skills, your interests, and your values. Their stories will motivate you to carry out an effective job search campaign, because you'll know it's worth it.

Each of the Real People advises you to gain real work experience, either through internships or work, to prepare for your profession. Chances are, you'll find relevant opportunities if you talk to people in your network. **A key benefit of work and internships is the connections you'll make that can expand your network.**

After obtaining your first job out of college, don't neglect your network. With an active network, you may never have to job hunt again. People will call you when they hear about positions of interest to you.

Developing Networking Relationships

When you think of networking, you may picture someone at a meeting shaking hands and passing his business card to as many contacts as possible. The more people you connect with the better. To some extent, this is true; yet remember that the goal of networking is to develop and *maintain* relationships. Networking is sharing time, information, resources, and opportunities. **It's built on a simple but well-known principle: it's easier to get information and help from people who either know you or know someone who knows you than from people who have never heard of you.**

Although some people find the prospect of networking scary, it's a simple method that you already know how to do. You probably have developed a network at school—people you can call on when you've missed a class or need help understanding an assignment. In the process, you've probably learned a vital networking principle: to keep a relationship alive, it should benefit both people. Networking is crucial throughout your career, but when you are searching for work, it makes the difference between finding "just a job" and finding one that fits *you*.

The first step in developing a network is to start with the people you already know. Although you may think you've been too busy with school, work, and internships to develop a network, everyone knows people who can help them in their search for work. Every day, you meet and exchange information with many people. You'd be surprised who may know someone in your field or someone who works at a company where you'd like to work—it might even be your pal at Starbucks. You won't know unless you ask.

When you first start networking, particularly with professionals already in the field, you will be on the receiving end of the relationship. Try to find ways to keep the relationships active until you graduate so they can help you during your work search. While you are a student, you have access to the latest case studies, new start-up ideas, and other groundbreaking news. **There are several ways you can share this information with interested people in your network. You can send them a copy of a business article.** Another time-saving idea is to write your own "Cliffs Notes for Busy People." Summarize articles and e-mail them to your contacts. You may think people in your network are already reading these articles, but it's likely they haven't had time. Just because they have *Harvard Business Review* sitting on their desk doesn't mean they've actually had time to read it. It's also a good idea to keep them updated on your progress.

Send them a short note periodically telling them about a class you're enjoying or an internship you're doing. **Many marketing people say you should connect with people in your network once every 30 days.** Don't rely just on e-mail—occasionally give them a call to update them on your progress. Don't worry if you get voice mail, it's fine to just leave a cheery message that lets them know what you're doing.

Tip:
Even busy executives will respond to your call if you give them a valid reason. Use names, events, or news to show a connection.

Developing Relationships in College

College is the perfect time to begin developing professional contacts and relationships. Your campus is full of people who can provide essential information about the world of work, as well as connections when you begin your job search. Use the time while you're a student to polish your networking skills.

Your Peers

Nearly everyone you meet in college will one day be working, and some of them will be working in companies of interest to you—as potential suppliers, customers, or employers. You can build positive relationships with peers by sharing notes, studying for exams, and participating in joint class projects. Use these experiences to learn how to work with others, assert your viewpoint, and collaborate to achieve results. Stay in touch with classmates after graduation—you have already built a network that can lead you to others in your field. Sharing first-year work experiences will help each of you achieve success early in your career.

Program Advisors

The more your advisor knows about your work goals, the more she can help you select the courses most beneficial to you. Advisors are in touch with employers in your field of study, so they can provide you with contacts to help you learn more about work opportunities. Advisors may also be aware of internships, co-op experiences, and employers looking for job candidates.

Career Center Counselors

Most colleges have career centers where you can access information about career fields, internships, job-search techniques, and on-campus interviews. A career center counselor can help you find work related to your field while you're in school. Many career centers maintain useful Web sites linked to the campus home page. Although career center Web sites are useful, they cannot provide the personal relationship and insights that a counselor can.

The Buzz:
"Networking is very important when it's up to you to track down the companies you're interested in working for, and you have to find a way to get yourself invited for an interview. Using any connection you have is the best way to get your foot in the door at a company and get an interview. If you know someone who can make an introduction for you at a company, at least you can be sure that someone there will read your resumé. Sending an unsolicited resumé to a company's human resources department is the least effective way of getting yourself an interview."

Russell A. Boss, Member of the Board of Directors., A.T. Cross Company

Professors

Many students think to contact their instructors only when they're having trouble with an assignment. Professors, however, can also be invaluable in helping you prepare for your future career. **If you share your dreams with them, they can help you identify resources that will help you achieve your goals. Instructors serve on community boards, consult with businesses, and read numerous publications about workplace trends.**

Clubs

Your campus has many clubs for students to learn more about careers in particular fields. **Clubs and professional organizations also provide a setting where you can develop relationships with peers who will be working in your profession.**

Identify Your Network

Instructions: Using the categories below, write the names of at least 25 people who are members of your network. Don't worry about addresses and phone numbers now; you can look those up later. Stretch your mind to list as many people as possible, including teachers, advisors, friends of your parents, bank tellers, auto mechanics, and so on.

Group	Network Members
Family/friends—family members, neighbors, friends	
Acquaintances/neighborhood contacts—club members, church groups, community groups	
School—advisors, instructors, classmates	
Professional colleagues—former bosses, current and former co-workers, association members, customers, suppliers	
Service providers—doctors, lawyers, hair stylists, mechanics, trainers	
Volunteer work/internships—community groups, contacts from internships	

Ways to Expand Your Network

The key to starting a new networking relationship: communicate a mutual interest and a valid reason for connecting with the person. (Hmmm . . . sounds a lot like dating!) Even busy executives will take your call if your appeal is legitimate. For example, Jim Lawrence, vice president for Darden Restaurants speaks at seminars at Cornell University. He says a student in the seminar can seek his advice by following up afterward. He states, "If they have a good reason for meeting with me, I'll find the time. I've given tours and advice to students who have contacted me in this way. After all, they are potential customers, stockholders, or employees, so it's in Darden's interests for me to be helpful."

No matter how many people you know, you may need additional ways to connect with people who have the inside scoop on your industry sector or profession. The following ideas will help:

- **Join a professional association.** Many associations have student chapters on campus or offer reduced rates for student members. All of them welcome students or new graduates aspiring to work in their profession. Go to the Internet library, **www.ipl.org/div/AON** for a searchable directory of business-related associations.

- **Talk to speakers at conferences and professional meetings.** Call ahead and ask conference speakers if they have time to meet with you after their presentations. Many conferences need volunteers to help with logistics at the event. They will usually waive the conference fee in exchange for help. You'll still have time to attend presentations and meet attendees.

- **E-mail or call authors of articles in trade journals or magazines.** Authors spend time writing to gain visibility and recognition. They appreciate hearing from people who have read their material, and they may have good ideas about other people you could talk to about your job search.

- **Inform your favorite bloggers about your search.** Blog hosts are often leaders in their industry, so they have many contacts. Although they may not post your inquiry, they may be willing to share information with you if you ask. To appeal to their generous side, start your query with a statement about why you enjoy reading their blog.

- **Reach out to your Facebook or other social network and ask for people you can contact for help with your search.** Keep expanding your network so you can ask questions about professions, industries, and companies and get good information. Note: First, be sure your social networking pages are appropriate for business contacts. The pictures of the spring break trip are probably not what you want your prospective employer to see.

- **Join professional social networks such as www.linkedin.com.** Create your profile and find people in your preferred industry and make connections.

Keep in Touch
Send holiday and birthday cards to the people with whom you network. It's a thoughtful way and a great reason to touch base.

Get Connected
There are many professional social networks which provide an opportunity for you to connect with people in your target industry. Here are a few to consider:

www.linkedin.com
www.jobster.com
www.biznik.com
www.ryze.com
www.ecademy.com
www.womanowned.com

Ways to Expand Your Network

Instructions: List below the ways you will expand your network. Include names of people or groups you can contact.

_____

_____

_____

_____

_____

_____

_____

_____

_____

_____

_____

_____

Connecting with Your Network during Your Work Search

Networking is *not* asking for a job; it's asking for information to help with your job search. You may not personally know anyone who works at a company on your list of possible employers, but the people you do know can get you closer to your target.

Use Your Value Proposition

Once you've identified the people in your network, what do you say to them? That's easy—just tell them your value proposition! It's a ready-made marketing tool that is compelling and to the point. **You may revise your proposition depending on your audience, but every communication should include something about how you can solve employer needs.** In addition, let each person know what you are looking for, and the kind of support you'd like from her. For example, you might want to ask if the

Tip: Don't Discount *Anyone* as a Possible Resource!
After attending college and working a few years in California, Sarah decided to move back to her hometown. As she dropped off her dry cleaning one day, Sarah mentioned to the clerk that she was looking for a job as a chemist in a research lab. The clerk's brother worked at just such a facility and she offered to call him for Sarah. The result? She got the job!

person knows anyone who works in a particular industry sector or at a company where you'd like to work. Use a script like the following:

> "Hello, this is _____. As you know, I'll be graduating in June with my degree in marketing. I'm really excited about using my writing and research skills in product marketing. I'm calling to see if you know anyone who works at _____ company. I'd like to ask them a few questions about the company."

or

> "I'm calling to see if you know anyone who works in the field. I'd like to ask them a few questions about their background."

Another way to connect with people in your network is to send them an e-mail. **Write your value proposition in the body of your e-mail along with the kind of help you'd like.** Use the NAB approach discussed in Chapter 13 so the addressee can see what you have to offer at a glance. Again, be specific—make it easy for people to help you. If you attach your resumé people may forward it to their colleagues.

Ask for a Meeting

Make a list of all the contacts you've received from your network or other resources. You will have the most impact if you can meet them in person. You will find it much easier to connect with a person you don't know if you use the name of the person who referred you.

Often the best strategy is to e-mail the reason for wanting to connect, stating that you'll call in the next two days. Place the call and ask for a meeting. If they can't meet in person, ask questions over the phone. That's better than no information at all.

When you call, use a script like one of the following:

> "Hello, my name is _____. I spoke with _____ about working in the field of _____. S/he recommended I contact you because of your background in _____. I'm wondering if I could spend 15 minutes talking to you about your experience. I'd like your advice about what I should do to get started in this field. When would it be convenient to meet with you?"

or

> "Hello, my name is _____. I enjoyed your presentation at the student AMA meeting. I was particularly interested in what you had to say about _____. This is an interest of mine too. I'll be

Networking That Works

Always include a modified version of your cover letter in the text of the e-mail when you are sending your resumé to someone who requested it. Chances are that person will be forwarding your resumé to someone else and every recipient can clearly see what you have to offer without an additional click.

graduating in June and would be appreciate your advice about careers related to _____. When would it be convenient to meet with you?"

Think about what you want to achieve during the meeting. Here are some possibilities:

- Learn what skills, training, and entry-level or part-time experience would help you enter the field.
- Get suggestions about ways to acquire needed skills or experience.
- Obtain job-hunting advice for this field.
- Learn *insider* information about an organization. Ask the person to describe the company culture and the kind of person who thrives there.
- Obtain feedback on your resumé or your interviewing style and other job-hunting advice.

Research the company before you meet with the person. Become familiar with the company's products and services, organizational structure, and competitors. Candidates who don't bother to do their homework don't appear genuinely interested in the company. Your research will demonstrate your motivation as a professional job seeker.

Ask for Advice, Not a Job

If you ask for a job, particularly over the phone, it's easy for the other person to say no. **If you ask for advice, most people are flattered and will usually agree to meet with you.** Ask whether they prefer to meet at a nearby coffee shop or their office.

Prepare for each interview by developing a list of questions to ask. Summarize your background by using your value proposition. It is fine to have your questions written down and to take notes during the meeting—it will create a professional impression.

Your questions during the networking interview differ from research interviews because you have already decided on a profession or industry. Now, you are using the law of averages to your advantage: The more people you talk to, the more likely you will be in the right place at the right time—when an opening exists.

Possible questions to ask include:

- How did you get started in this profession?
- What kinds of skills are most important in your work?
- What kinds of problems do you solve?
- What types of experience are needed for working in this field?
- What advice would you give someone entering this career?
- **Would you recommend other people I could talk to about work in this field? (Always, always ask this question.)**

Secret Strategy:
Ask every person you talk to for the names of two or three other people she recommend you speak to. It will expand your network exponentially and you'll be using a referral instead of making a cold call.

Say Thank You.
Send a personal e-mail or handwritten note to each person within 24 hours.

Build on the information you gather, and follow up with your contacts to keep them posted on your progress. Check the validity of ideas you've heard by asking others about them. For example: "Sally Brown at XYZ Company suggested I start by working through a temporary agency. Do you agree? What agency does your company use?"

A Word of Caution

If you told the person on the phone that you were seeking information, don't turn the tables and ask for a job. The person will feel used and they won't want to help you at all. If there are openings at the company for which you qualify, she will let you know.

My Career Journal

Recruiters consistently say they prefer candidates who have internship or work experience. It's best if that experience is related to their career field. Who in your network could help you find an internship or part-time work to help you gain that experience now?

_____

_____

_____

_____

_____

_____

_____

Plan at least one informational meeting to learn more about the career field you are considering. What resources will you use to find a person to talk to?

_____

_____

_____

_____

_____

_____

_____

_____

List below the questions you will ask that person.

_____

_____

_____

_____

_____

_____

Notes to Myself

Delivering Your Value Proposition

Step 5

Going on interviews and evaluating job offers might seem far off right now, but be prepared. They will happen sooner than you think.

When it's time for a face-to-face meeting with your prospective employer, you want to be as prepared as possible in every way. You've done a lot of work to get the interview, now you want to turn it into a job offer. Learn the ins and outs of interviewing so you can get the internship or full-time job you want.

It's exciting to receive a job offer. But before you accept it, do you know everything you need to know about the company, the job, and the compensation? What if you are interviewing with two companies and receive an offer from one but really want the offer from the other one? What if you receive two job offers, how do you determine which one is really better?

Read Chapters 15 and 16 now. And reread them again before each interview. Every time you read them, you will feel more confident, ask better questions, learn more about negotiating a job offer, and even enjoy the process.

Welcome to the Real World! ➤

15
Delivering Value:
How to Make Every Interview Successful

Objectives

1. How should I prepare for job interviews?

2. How can I stand out among all the candidates?

3. What kinds of questions can I expect?

4. What should I wear to an interview?

Wouldn't it be great if employers automatically recognized the contributions you can make? Unfortunately, they don't. Perhaps you're thinking, "I'm completing my education, so I'll have a diploma to get my foot in the door." Your education, although important, won't bring employers to you. And no matter how extensive your network or how dynamic your resumé, those things won't get the job for you either. It's up to you to let people know what you have to offer.

No doubt about it. Searching for work is a form of relationship selling. After all, you and the hiring manager will have a long-term relationship if you are successful. The manager wants to get to know you personally and discuss your abilities. He wants to assess whether you have what it takes to do the job and how you will fit in with their corporate culture. You don't need slick answers or a hard sell. **By promoting your strengths and describing how you can add value to the department, you will be able to convince an employer who offers the kind of opportunity you're seeking.**

A seasoned salesperson doesn't call on a potential customer without preparation. Salespeople find out as much as they can about their client's history, buying habits, and product needs. They thoroughly plan their presentation, focusing on the benefits that will appeal most to this particular customer. With preparation, a sales pro enters the customer meeting with confidence.

You can act like a seasoned pro by using the personal selling process outlined in *Marketing: Real People, Real Choices.* By applying each step, you'll be well prepared by the time you step into an interview.

Prospecting and Qualifying

You have already learned how to research your industry in Chapter 4 and how to put together your integrated marketing communication plan in Chapter 12. That is your process for prospecting and qualifying. Use the target company list you created in Activity 12.1 as your list of qualified prospects.

Even for experienced professionals, job hunting is an emotional rollercoaster ride. Some days you'll soar with anticipation and hope. Other days you'll find your confidence slipping after a rejection. Everyone needs resiliency during a job search. You'll find it much easier to keep up your momentum if you have several prospects in the works. Your list of companies will keep you on track—you'll already know whom to pursue next. **Inexperienced job hunters often make the mistake of singling out one employer at a time.** Instead, you want to do what experienced salespeople do. You will achieve success sooner if you develop a comprehensive job-search campaign, working on a mix of activities at any one time. Even while you're interviewing with one employer, stay connected to your network and send out resumés to other firms in your target market.

Preapproach

Success! You've researched companies, written your resumé, implemented your communication plan, networked, and now your hard work has paid off—you've been invited for an interview. Once you've made it to this stage, you know the employer is interested in you. Now it's time to close the deal.

Get a Complete Job Description

The way to stand out from the competition is to gather background information about the specific position so you can plan your interview. You want to know everything you can about the job. Most people don't think to call the company, but you can call the human resources department and request a full job description. This is important because many job postings sometimes show only the highlights of the requirements—a full job description gives the details. When you call, the person answering your request may also be willing to give you "insider" information that you can use in the interview. Ask about new company initiatives, new management, or new products—anything you can discuss in the interview to show that you've done your homework and have learned about the culture you hope to join.

Stand Out

Set up a Google News alert, at **www.news.google.com**, for each of your target companies. That way you will know about any breaking news and will be able to talk about it during the interview.

Research the Company On-line

What should you know about the company? You can find key information about most companies by going to the company Web site, doing an Internet search or going to **www.hoovers.com**. Your campus library may have a subscription. Here are some of the basic facts employers expect you to know:

- How many locations and employees does the company have?
- What are the key products or services offered by the company?
- Are their customers other businesses or consumers?
- How long has the company been in business? Have they merged or been acquired recently?
- How does the company's market share they compare to that of competitors?
- Does the company have new any products or services? Is the company expanding globally?
- Have the CEO or others received awards or published a book or article recently?

Prepare Your Interview Questions

Inevitably, you'll be asked if *you* have any questions. Even though you may have questions about salary and benefits, **don't** ask about them at this time. (Review Chapter 16 for advice on how to negotiate.) Show your interest in the job by preparing great questions to ask in the interview. These questions show that you've thought about the position and the company. Here are some questions to consider asking:

- What would the ideal person for this position be like?
- What are some challenges facing the department in the next 90 days? What role will the person in this position play in tackling those challenges?
- How will the person be involved in the rollout of your new product?
- How would you describe the company culture?
- How would you describe your management style?
- Is there anything else about my background you'd like to know?
- What are the next steps in the hiring process?

The Best Interview Preparation
Practice!
Practice!
Practice!

After the interviewer responds to your questions, follow up by restating your strengths. For example, suppose the interviewer tells you the ideal person would be committed to achieving goals and learning new skills. Follow up by telling about a specific time when you achieved a goal or discuss how much you've enjoyed learning as a college student.

Prepare Your Key Selling Points

An interview is a sales call. You want to be prepared with the key selling points for your brand.

During the interview, your objective is to be sure the interviewer knows what you have to offer while answering his questions.

Read the section titled NAB the Interview by Telling Memorable Stories. Learn how to use NAB (Need, Action, Benefit) to make your brand come alive in interviews.

The key is to keep your NAB stories short, conversational, and focused. **Keep rehearsing them until they come naturally to you.**

Get Directions

Get directions to where you are going including building and floor. Be sure you are familiar with the travel time, especially during rush hours. Find out about parking or public transportation. Allow extra time for transportation.

Approach

The first few minutes of the interview are critical! **Approach your interviewer with a smile, a firm handshake, and eye contact.** Start off by finding ways to break the ice and establish rapport. You might mention something you've learned about the company (perhaps their new product is just now hitting the market). Or you can bring up something personal, like interesting items on the interviewer's desk. You'll feel more comfortable if you can get the interviewer to talk about himself for a few minutes before jumping into the questions.

We make quick judgments about people we meet for the first time; interviewers are no exception. **That's why it's important to dress professionally, make eye contact, and wear a big smile.**

Sales Presentation

An astonishing thing often happens when searching for work—people who are normally articulate start to falter and stammer the minute they hear those famous four words: "Tell me about yourself." It even happens to experienced people!

Perhaps it would be easier if you could just go in and give a sales presentation, laying out the benefits of your abilities. But that's not the way an interview works. **You do want to focus on your benefits; however, you must do that in response to questions.** Interviewing takes more preparation than a regular sales presentation because you have to be able to think on your feet. You have to figure out how to relate the points you want to make to the questions you're asked. **So the number one interviewing rule is to *overprepare.*** You want to walk into that interview knowing everything you possibly can about the company, the position, and today's business news. **In addition, you want to be prepared to confidently discuss how you will add value to the organization.**

Be Prepared

Bring a few extra copies of your resumé printed on 24-lb. paper in a folder or portfolio. Even though the interviewer already has your resumé, it might not be handy at the time of the interview. Or, you might be asked to meet with someone who was not originally on the interview schedule.

Smile!

Nothing is better for building rapport.

Last-Minute Check

Arrive early and ask the receptionist to use the rest room. Take a quick look to be sure your hair is in place, your clothes are straightened, and use a breath mint. Bring along a business publication such as the *Wall Street Journal* in case you have to wait.

Handling Objections

You won't hear objections during a job interview. Managers and recruiters are trained to remain neutral, and they rarely give feedback about how you're doing. They may follow up a question by probing for more information. That may be a cue that they're very interested in you. Or it could just mean that your answers are not specific enough. If you're going on lots of interviews and not getting job offers, you might try to get feedback from an interviewer. It is rare that they will be candid, however—interviewers are wary of discrimination lawsuits. A better way to get feedback is to ask a professional in your network to practice with you. **Some college career centers offer workshops on interviewing skills and videotape mock interviews.** This is a very good way to see how you're doing.

The Close

Close

Summarize your strengths and ask for the job!

Every sales situation involves a close—the point at which the salesperson asks the customer to commit to a purchase. **Most job seekers fail to close the interview.** An example of an appropriate close would be, "After the research I did before coming in, I was interested in working for your company. Now that I have a better understanding of the job and the advantages of working for your company, I'm even more excited about it. I would really like the opportunity to contribute to your success." **No matter what your impression is at this point, it is important to let the interviewer know you want the job.** The interview is not the time to make a decision about whether you'll accept the position. You can always say no if it is offered to you. But it may not be offered at all if you don't ask for it.

Say Thank You

Always send a thank-you note within 24 hours of an interview. An e-mail note is acceptable, but a hand-written note makes you stand out.

See sample thank-you notes in the *Brand You* Toolkit.

Follow up

No matter how well your interview went, it's important to follow up in order to seal the deal. **The first thing to do is to write a thank-you note within 24 hours.** A handwritten note is best, but an e-mail written as a letter has become acceptable. In your note

- thank the interviewer for his time and information;
- refer to something specific in the interview—a mutual contact, some connection with the interviewer, or a topic you discussed;
- briefly describe the key reasons you feel you are a good match for the position;
- reiterate your interest in the job; and
- be sincere.

Be sure to send a thank-you note to each person with whom you interviewed. In addition, send a thank-you note to the person who arranged the interview if it was not the interviewer. And, if you asked someone to be a reference for you, be sure to send that person or persons a thank-you note. Review the Sample Thank-You Notes in the *Brand You* Toolkit.

Call in about a week if you haven't heard from the employer. Just ask the status of his decision. Often pressing business matters interrupt the hiring process. Your phone call will send a signal regarding your interest and motivation. You don't want to become a pest; on the other hand, it's okay to check in once a week to ask about the progress. It's always better to know where you stand than to wonder what is happening.

Advice Straight from the Recruiter

- "Can I work with this person? Do they fit in with our corporate culture? These are the two questions that are in my mind when I interview. I use scenarios to see how the person responds to actual events. I select candidates who show enthusiasm, strong interpersonal skills, and good judgment when answering questions."—R. Bresnahan, manager for a large nonprofit organization

- "I look for a person's ability to solve logical problems. I want real-world experience (school experience isn't enough). The person must be good at verbal and written communications and be able to work independently because I'm a hands-off manager."—Anonymous manager

- "First, seriously assess yourself—strengths, weaknesses, and preferences. Second, research prospective employers. Third, don't put on an act you can't sustain day in and day out if hired."—Manager at a major chemical corporation

- "Learn how to dress, speak, WRITE!"—R. Gately, President, Gately Consulting

- "Be sincere, ask questions when you are confused, don't play hardball, and read a book on interview tips. Don't talk about drinking or sex habits, and keep clean the night before an interview. I have had people come in late and hung over. They think because I'm young that I would laugh. They were wrong."—HR Representative of a *Fortune* 500 electronics company.

Jim
Lawrence's Brand

You met Jim in **Chapter 15** *of* Marketing: Real People, Real Choices. *He's Senior Vice President of Supply Management and Purchasing for Darden Restaurants.*

▼ **Q** & **A** with Jim Lawrence

Key word:
Team player.

Distinctive competency:
A "Can do, whatever it takes" attitude.

My message:
Let's collaborate. I'm always looking for ways to build consensus so that everyone is engaged and empowered in the decision-making process. Focus on people, and the results will come.

One value I create for the company:
Never being satisfied with the status quo. Either you are moving forward or you are moving backward.

Jim's Advice

To prepare for the workplace:
Focus on obtaining leadership skills and experiences inside and outside the classroom. Building consensus and influencing others can be done in study groups, student government organizations, social organizations, etc. Many students focus so much on the product (grades) that they forget about the learning that is associated with the process.

A job-hunting strategy I would definitely use:
Develop a network of contacts. Students have a wide range of personal contacts by the time that they graduate from college. Cultivate relationships so that they can be used for job searching.

How a student can overcome lack of experience:
Internships are a great way to solve this issue. If for whatever reason, an internship is not feasible, try volunteering at a nonprofit organization. Students should always be searching to gain experiences that will translate to the work world.

The benefit of a personal brand:
Developing a personal brand requires self awareness, which is the first step toward personal improvement and development. Having a focused understanding of your strengths and developmental opportunities is vital to one's success.

NAB the Interview with Memorable Stories

Interviewers want to know about your accomplishments and the results you achieved. Many applicants give answers that are too general. They list personal skills and characteristics. After listening to five applicants in a row say they're dependable, hardworking, flexible, and a team player, the interviewer's eyes begin to glaze over—everyone sounds the same. These adjectives are not action words. They don't sound convincing and don't show your potential benefit to the company.

How can you stand out from the other applicants? How can you convince the interviewer you can solve his problems? By using storytelling narratives to illustrate what you can do.

The interviewer will remember personal real-life stories. **Your stories provide the context in which you used skills and show that you are a person who takes action to achieve results.** A positive side effect of telling stories is that you take yourself back to a time when you were with people you like and were accomplishing something important. The retelling will relax you and at least temporarily take your mind away from the stress of the interview.

A word of caution is needed here. We're talking about storytelling because stories create interest for the listener. However, we are not talking about fiction! Your stories should be factual, used to illustrate that you have accomplished things relevant to the employer's needs.

To create your memorable stories, complete a NAB (Need, Action, Benefit) worksheet like the one you wrote to develop your resumé. Dedicated candidates who want several offers from which to choose have found that NAB is the secret to acing an interview. They complete a NAB worksheet prior to each interview. From their cache of experiences, they select stories that relate to the specific needs of each employer.

Here's how to use the NAB worksheet to prepare for an interview. In the Needs column, write the knowledge, skills, and abilities mentioned in the job description. For each entry in your Action column, create a story that explains the situation thoroughly. Be sure to clearly describe what you did and emphasize the results you achieved. Whenever possible, quantify the results (for example, "We increased profits by 10 percent"). You might want to write the story first. Then practice telling the story until you can say it clearly. The final step is to look at the Frequently Asked Interview Questions described later in this chapter. Decide which of your stories would be a good answer for each question.

Become a Storyteller
Use NAB (Need, Action, Benefit) to stand out from the competition.

Sample Stories

Notice that this person doesn't have experience with trade shows, but tells an interesting story about a time when he used similar skills. A much stronger response than admitting he doesn't have experience!

How would you handle working at a trade show?

"I think I would be good at representing your products at trade shows—I like talking to people and giving them information. When I was a member of a campus club, we went door-to-door asking people to vote for local candidates. As a group, we decided which neighborhoods were the most critical. I helped write the script we used and kept everyone's motivation up on the days we canvassed. We met our goals in less time than we expected. I enjoyed talking to people about our candidates' views on the issues—I think I convinced a number of people to vote for them. I'm sure these are the same skills you would need to talk to potential customers at a trade show."

Tell me about a time when you worked on a team.

This story has lots of detail about a group project. She assumed a leadership role and helped another student succeed. A compelling story—the fact that it's a school project instead of a work team doesn't matter.

"One of my favorite classes was a class on market trends and research. The professor assigned us to teams. Our assignment was to write and present a market research project. Our group chose distance learning for college students. In the beginning, we had so many ideas about how we could do this that we couldn't focus very well. I volunteered to lead our discussions so we could decide on a plan of action and get busy on the project. People in the group seemed relieved that someone took charge. I made sure everyone had input into our decisions, but I didn't allow the group to waste time either. We had one member who wasn't contributing much at first. I talked to him privately and together we identified a part of the project that he was interested in doing. In the end, he developed all the visuals that really added to our presentation. We developed some innovative ways to research our topic, and we gathered comprehensive information. There was a lot of interest from the class when we made our presentation—and we got an A on our project!"

Keep Your Preparation Simple

Internet sites have lengthy articles filled with numerous interviewing techniques. Although it's mostly good advice, it can be overwhelming, and impossible to remember everything during the stress of an interview. **So keep it simple. Develop six great stories based on your NAB worksheet.** Bring each story to life by filling in the details and making it interesting. Practice your stories until you can say them without hesitation. In the interview, look for ways to transition from a question into your story. With these six great responses, you'll demonstrate commitment and enthusiasm.

Stories are compelling because they are remembered. When the interviewer is evaluating all the candidates, he'll remember your stories and be able to put your face with the interview.

Identifying Organizational Culture

Instructions: Knowing the culture of an organization can help you prepare for your interview. The information will help you decide what to say and even what to wear. Brainstorm with a group of fellow students. Select an actual company in your chosen field and create a list of resources you can use to identify the organization's culture. List what you found from each resource (split this up and report back if necessary).

	Company	Organizational Culture
Resource 1		
Resource 2		
Resource 3		
Resource 4		
Resource 5		

How to Handle Behavioral Interviews

Many managers use an interviewing approach called *behavioral interviewing.* It is based on the premise that past behavior most likely predicts future behavior. Thus, if you've demonstrated the skill or knowledge in the past, you will do it at this company, too. Interviewers are looking for positive behaviors—real-time examples of things you've done—not generalities, traits, or personality characteristics.

Behavioral interviewing questions start with, "Tell me about a time when. . ." or "Give me an example of. . ." Interviewers then continue to probe and ask questions about this particular experience until they have a clear, realistic picture of the event. **You'll be a star if you respond with one of your prepared answers, using one of your NAB (Need, Action, Benefit) experiences to paint a picture of your accomplishments.** Always describe the results you achieved and their benefit. Choose situations with positive outcomes. If you're asked to describe a stressful experience, talk about the event in a positive, upbeat manner.

Keep It Simple
Develop six great NAB (Need, Action, Benefit) stories and practice them until they're perfect. Then think about the kinds of questions for which you can use them.

Tell Your Story
Give specific descriptions of past events—don't talk in generalities.

Take time to organize your thoughts before answering a question. You don't want to ramble or appear off track. **It's okay to say, "Let me think about that for a minute." It's also okay to ask a question if you don't understand something.** You may be asked to describe the situation in greater detail, as the interviewer looks for examples of specific behaviors. If you've studied the job description, you'll know the behaviors they're looking for, and you'll be able to include them in your response.

With this style of interviewing, the recruiter strives to create a comfortable environment, encouraging the applicant to describe and tell more. Beware of becoming too comfortable and saying things you will regret later. **Even though recruiters may seem very friendly, they are still evaluating your responses.** Always give a favorable impression. We've heard stories of people who described how they told off their last boss or went over the heads of their teachers to get their grades improved. Another applicant told the interviewer he was getting married in a few months and would be moving to another city. There is nothing wrong with leaving a job after a short time, but don't bring it up in the interview.

Frequently Asked Interview Questions—And How to Answer Them

Although it's impossible to predict the questions you'll be asked, practice answering these typical questions. The secret to a great interview is to be prepared to discuss your skills and how you can benefit the company. Your NAB stories will do this for you. **Remember to practice your answers out loud—things that sound good in your head are often missing key words!**

Interview Question	How to Answer
Tell me about yourself.	Interviewers often ask this broad question to build rapport and begin the interview. Launch your value proposition. Focus your answer on your skills and interest in the field, giving a brief chronological overview. Avoid discussing personal or family information.
Tell me about a time when you achieved more than was expected.	The interviewer wants to know about your personal commitment to a task. How motivated are you? Are you results-oriented? Do you inspire others? How have you shown initiative in the past? Use examples from your education or work experience. The recruiter is most interested in the behaviors you exhibited to achieve a particular goal.

Continue on the next page...

Interview Question	How to Answer
Describe a time when you had a conflict with someone.	You can't avoid this question by saying you've never been involved in a conflict. Everyone has conflicts. The interviewer wants to know how you handle and resolve them. What happened and how did you react? Are you the kind of person who blows up and adds fuel to the fire, tries different ways to keep peace, or avoids conflict and walks away? Your answer should describe a time when you successfully resolved conflict in a reasonable and appropriate way. Choose a small conflict at work or school, and focus on what you did to resolve the problem.

When asked this question, the most recent or troubling conflict you've experienced might pop into your head. Don't describe these situations or any issues that you feel emotional about and avoid talking about parents, roommates, or spouses. You want to appear rational and even-tempered. Stay away from blaming or berating anyone. Instead, discuss an issue like differences in work styles, and describe how you resolved the problem. Don't pick a situation you walked away from, such as dropping a class or quitting a job. |
Give me an example of a time when you had to work under pressure.	The recruiter wants to know how you handle stress and deadlines. What do you consider stressful? Can you meet deadlines? Do you thrive under pressure or buckle under deadlines? Describe a situation with pressure that has to do with deadlines rather than personalities of co-workers. Talk about strategies you successfully used to stay calm.
Tell me about a time when you dealt with an angry customer.	The interviewer wants to know how you react to angry people. Do you use different strategies to calm irate people? Do you do everything you can to make sure customers walk away happy? Do you strictly enforce company policies or often bend them to keep customers coming back? Talk about an exchange that ended positively—a time when you successfully calmed an angry customer and resolved the situation. Don't use examples in which you referred an angry customer to others.
Describe a situation when you analyzed a problem and arrived at a solution.	The recruiter wants to evaluate your decision-making skills. Did you use a systematic approach or intuition? Were you impulsive, or did you delay and overanalyze the problem? Choose a situation that you systematically analyzed, and describe how you handled it.
What are your strengths?	The interviewer looks to see if your strengths match the skills needed in the position. Use this opportunity to talk about your strengths that are related to the job. Give examples of times when you demonstrated them. Describe skills by using one or two of your NAB experiences.
What are your weaknesses?	This question is used to assess your self-confidence. Pick a real weakness (but not your worst one!) and then describe how you overcame it. For example, "I sometimes volunteer to take on too many tasks because I see they need to be done. When this happens, I may ask my supervisor to help me prioritize them." Don't talk about problems with past bosses, co-workers, or roommates.
Why do you want to work for this company?	This question seeks to find out what you know about the company. It gives you the opportunity to show you have done your research. Don't just say "it's a great company that's growing." Instead, look the interviewer in the eye and say, "I really want to work for your company because. . . ." Talk about what you can do to solve a problem or add value to the team. One recruiter told us, "We asked an applicant why she wanted to work for our company. Her reply, 'It must be a good company to work for' wasn't enough and I didn't hire her. I think anyone should be able to express why they want the job they are applying for."

Continue on the next page...

Interview Question	How to Answer
Why should I hire you?	Tell specifically how you can be an asset to this organization, and let the interviewer know that you want to work there (even if you're not sure yet). You would be surprised how many applicants never ask directly for the job.
What did you like best about your last job?	Focus on similarities between that job and this one. Share another NAB experience.
What did you like least about your last job?	The interviewer is hoping you will reveal conflicts—don't do it. Beware of complaining! A basic principle of job-hunting is to never say anything negative about a former employer. So you could answer: "I enjoyed my work at XYZ Company, but I guess one thing I didn't like was. . . ." Pick something that is not critical in the job for which you are applying. End your response on a positive note by talking about your readiness for new challenges.
Where do you see yourself in five years?	The recruiter wants to know if you set goals and plan to keep learning. Talk about skills you can reasonably learn in this position and responsibilities you could meet as a result. Don't talk about promotions within the company or long-term employment—that may not be in the cards. Don't mention returning to school full-time or any plans that might indicate a short commitment to the employer.
What was your favorite class in college?	Describe a class related to the type of work for which you are interviewing. Tell about relevant class activities, assignments, and group projects you enjoyed.

Dress for Success

Think Twice about Your First Impression

"When a candidate asks me what to wear, I tell him or her that you only have one chance to make a good first impression. You decide."—A public relations executive for a major sports and entertainment company.

What's the best way to dress for an interview? Unless you are interviewing for a job to be a rock star, keep it professional.

Dressing for success can be challenging in today's casual work environment. Some industries are more formal than others and every company is different. You never know what the environment is until you get there. You can ask the person who is arranging the interview about what to wear. However, even if that person says the dress code is casual or business casual, be prepared to dress for success.

You might be tempted to dress for the environment, but it's more important to dress for success. When in doubt, dress professionally. No matter what the profession, you can't go wrong dressing professionally or conservatively; you can make a mistake dressing too casually or too trendy. You can always dress down after you get the job. Even if you are interviewing in a more casual industry such as advertising, position yourself as the professional you are. A public relations executive for a major sports and entertainment company said it best, "When a candidate asks me what to wear, I tell him or her that you only have one chance to make a good first impression. You decide."

Here are a few guidelines:

Women: Professional Dress

- Wear a professional dress or suit (skirt or pants with blazer) in a conservative color (black, beige, brown, or navy are best). Do not wear a sundress or dress with thin straps or low necklines. The hemline should be at or slightly above the knee.
- Your suit or dress should fit you well. If it's too tight or too loose, invest in a new one. You'll use it when you are working. If the suit or dress needs to be tailored, have it done. Fit makes you look and feel more confident.
- Wear conservative shoes or basic pumps in a neutral color with appropriate color hosiery. Leave the stilettos, platform shoes, and flip flops at home.
- Hair and makeup should look natural; no heavy eye shadow or bright lipstick.
- Wear appropriate accessories; no big bracelets, chandelier earrings, or large rings.
- No tattoos or body piercings should be visible other than pierced ears.
- Carry a professional handbag or briefcase; no back packs, please.

Women: Business Casual

- Same as above; you can be a bit more flexible with your color choices, but don't go overboard.

Men: Professional Dress

- Wear a suit in a conservative color (navy, gray, or black are best); white shirt and coordinating tie.
- Your suit should fit you well. If you don't have a good suit, invest in one and have it tailored to fit. You will use it when you start working. A well-fitting suit makes you look and feel more confident.
- Your shirt should fit you well and be pressed. A wrinkled shirt makes a bad impression.
- Wear polished conservative shoes in a color to complement your suit with appropriate color of hosiery.
- Don't wear any jewelry except a watch and ring.
- Tattoos or body piercings should not be visible.
- Carry a professional portfolio or briefcase; no back packs, please.

Men: Business Casual

- Wear a blazer (navy is the standard color for a blazer) and a shirt in white or a pale color with a coordinating tie.
- See notes above about fit and a pressed shirt.

- Wear appropriate shoes; nothing that resembles an athletic shoe, a sandal, or a flip flop.
- Wear appropriate color of socks.
- Don't wear jewelry except a watch and ring.
- Tattoos or body piercings should not be visible.
- Carry a professional portfolio or briefcase; no back packs, please.

Be ready for every interview by reviewing the Interview Checklist in the *Brand You* Toolkit.

My Career Journal

Go back to Chapter 9 and review your Value Proposition. How could you rephrase or change this statement to relate your features and benefits to the company you chose in Activity 15.1?

_____

_____

_____

_____

_____

Write a NAB (Need, Action, Benefit) statement to answer the following FAQs:

What are your strengths?

_____

_____

_____

_____

_____

What are your weaknesses?

_____

_____

_____

_____

_____

Give an example of a time when you worked under pressure. (Be sure to pick a time when you were successful!)

_____

_____

_____

_____

_____

Write down three questions you will ask on a job interview.

_____

_____

_____

_____

_____

Notes to **Myself**

16
Evaluating and Finalizing Your Offer:
Get What You Want

This is it! This is where it all comes together. You have gone on interviews, impressed your prospective employer, and now you are about to get a job offer. This step in your work search is just as important as each of the others. Even though it seems like you have arrived, don't relax just yet. Take the time to carefully read this chapter. Then, reread this chapter and complete the activities as soon as you receive a job offer. It's an exciting time, but don't get caught up in the excitement and miss something important. You don't want to be disappointed when you start your job.

Objectives

1. How do I determine if an offer is a good offer?
2. Can I negotiate a better offer?
3. What if I get one offer before another offer?
4. What do I need to do to accept the offer?
5. Do I need an offer letter for an internship or a full-time job?

Salary Discussions

For most people, salary is an important factor in evaluating a job offer. It shouldn't be your only consideration, especially if career satisfaction, flexibility, and lifestyle options are important to you. No matter where salary fits in your list of incentives, you'll wind up with the best possible compensation package if you understand how to discuss salary and how to negotiate it.

There are two basic principles that every job seeker should know:

1. Don't go to an interview without knowing what you're worth.
2. Delay discussion of salary as long as possible.

Although employers have a salary range for their open positions, you should calculate your market value. Study typical salaries for the job you're considering. Then analyze how you'll contribute to the profitability of the company. This analysis should be based on the value of your education, experience, and the responsibility of the position. Reread Chapter 11 – Pricing the Product to review resources you can use to establish your value.

Why should you delay salary discussions? Think about other sales situations. When a salesperson wants the consumer to buy a high-end product, she lays out all the features and benefits. She waits until she knows the consumer is sold on the product before she brings up cost. The best time to discuss salary is when both of you have a strong interest in one another.

Sometimes it's not possible to completely delay salary discussions. You may be asked to disclose your salary expectations in response to a job posting or in your first screening interview. Remember that you usually can't negotiate up from the lowest figure you name. Here's how you can handle these situations:

- In your cover letter, you can ignore the request. Or you can say, "I expect to earn market value for the responsibilities of the position." However, be aware that your resumé may be ignored if you don't provide a figure when asked (HR likes people who follow directions). **Never include salary expectations in your letter unless asked.**

- In the interview, one way to respond to a question about your salary expectations is to reply with a question of your own. You can ask, "What would a person with my background, skills, and qualifications typically earn at your company?"

- Sometimes the interviewer won't answer that question and will probe again for your requirements. Be as nonspecific as possible. "I know I can contribute value to your organization, but I'd like to wait until we're both sure I'm the right person for the job." Another possible response is to say, "I'm comfortable with the salary range you are offering. I'd like to discuss the specifics when I know more about the responsibilities of the job." If pressed to name an actual figure, respond with a broad range. Be sure you would accept the lowest figure in your range—that could be the one you are offered in the end.

If salary comes up at the end of the interview, thank the interviewer for making the offer. An appropriate response would be, **"Thank you for offering me the position. After learning more about your company and the responsibilities of the job, I'm excited about the opportunity to work for the XYZ Company. I'm sure I can make an impact and I'm ready to consider your best offer."** At this point, the employer may name a salary or provide a range. You can respond by saying, "This is within my expectations, depending on the entire package."

Usually the offer won't come during the interview. Instead, the hiring manager or recruiter will call you and make the offer later. Have paper and pen handy so you can take notes. When the offer is made, don't be afraid to ask questions to find out everything you need to know to evaluate the offer. That might include:

- What is the entire compensation package, including benefits?
- What exactly does the benefits package include?
- What are the opportunities for your personal development and promotion?
- When will your salary be reviewed? What do you need to do to earn at a higher level?
- What salary increases can you expect in three to five years?
- Is the offer subject to any conditions, such as a background check, verification of work history, drug testing, or security clearance?

Regardless of whether you are offered the job in the interview or on the phone, don't accept immediately. Tell the person offering the job, **"Thank you for offering me a position with your company. I'd like a little time to consider your offer. May I call you back later this week?"** New college grads have a tendency to be so grateful for employment, that they don't take time to evaluate the offer. This is an important decision for both you and the employer. Now that they've offered you the job, they want an enthusiastic employee, not someone who accepted only because she couldn't say no. Employers don't expect you to answer immediately—they won't withdraw the offer if you ask for a few days to consider it. So take time to evaluate whether this is the right job for you

No Secrets
Don't be afraid to ask about details of a job offer. It's a good idea to ask for a copy of the company benefits package to be sure you understand every benefit that is offered...or not offered. And, it's very acceptable (and usually encouraged) to call back the company while you are considering your offer to get additional information about the offer. Use the evaluation sheet in Activity 16.1 as a guide as to what questions to ask.

Evaluating the Offer

It's hard to turn down an offer for a job, especially if your search has taken a long time, but you want to be confident that you'll be happy in your new position. No matter how excited you are, it pays to sit back and assess the match between you and the work. Think back to the activities you completed at the beginning of this book. Is this the industry where you want to be right now? Is this the specialty in which you want to start paying your dues? How will you feel in a year when you see this job on your updated resumé?

If a salary seems higher than you'd expect, there's probably a reason for it. Here are reasons why companies sometimes pay more than the industry average:

- The company is fast-paced and demands long hours.
- They have a retention problem and think money is a way to keep people.
- The boss is hard to work for.
- They really do value employees and want to retain good workers.

Find out which reason applies—you can do that in the interview with good questions. Then decide if you can live with the consequences.

The best way to see how the offer adds up is to complete Activities 16.1 and 16.2.

One mistake new grads often make is to fail to take into account the benefits that are offered. If you're like many people starting your career, you might think you're invincible and you'll never get sick. But health and life insurance are important and expensive. Health plans and other benefits actually represent a hefty chunk in the equation—they often equal 30 percent of your pay. **Even if you can't negotiate salary, companies will often increase benefits if you ask for them.**

Employee benefits vary from company to company. Many offer a cafeteria plan of benefits, allowing employees to choose what they like best from a variety of options. Benefits are constantly changing as companies scramble to remain competitive. Here are some of the most common benefits about which you should ask:

- **Vacation, sick leave, personal holidays, and time off.** Many companies now lump together vacation, personal holidays, sick leave, and time off, calling it *paid time off*, and you can use it as you wish. (Personal holidays are paid days off that you can take when you want. Holidays are paid holidays that fall on major federal holidays such as Fourth of July, Thanksgiving, Christmas, etc.) You may be able to negotiate another week of vacation in lieu of higher salary. Be sure to ask when you are eligible to use the vacation, sick leave, time off, and personal holidays.
- **Health insurance.** Most companies provide medical insurance for full-time employees. Companies may pay a percentage of health insurance costs for employees and their families, and the employee pays the rest. Coverage can vary dramatically. Insurance options include medical savings accounts, HMOs, PPOs, dental, and vision.
- **Life insurance.** Term or whole life insurance may be offered. Usually the policy terminates when employment ends.
- **401(k) or pension plan.** A 401(k) plan allows you to build a tax-deferred retirement nest egg. Some employers match your contribution or a portion of it. Employer matching is a valuable benefit as it is additional income that is deposited in your 401(k) account. If a pension plan is offered, the employer puts money into a fund for your retirement.
- **Stock options (ESOPs).** This option allows the employee to buy a certain amount of company stock at a discounted price. Employees may buy the stock, pocketing the difference between the option price and the market price.
- **Signing bonus.** Bonuses have become a popular way to entice employees to join the company. They are commonly offered during good economic times or to high-demand employees. Typically, the bonus is paid to the employee upon successful completion of the probationary period or after one year.
- **Child care/elder care assistance.** Some companies offer on-site day care for children of employees. Other companies offer pretax savings accounts to meet child care or elder care expenses; the company may or may not contribute money to the account.
- **Tuition reimbursement.** This is an important benefit if you plan to pursue a graduate degree. Rules for reimbursement vary, so find out the company's policy.

Relocation Information

Before you accept a job which requires relocation, be sure you understand exactly which relocation costs will be paid by the company. Go to **www. rileyguide.com/relocate. html** to find out what you can expect.

Compensation Comparison Worksheet

Instructions: When you receive a job offer (or offers), fill in the information next to each compensation element to objectively evaluate the offer (or offers). Use this worksheet to evaluate one offer or to compare multiple offers.

Compensation Element	Job Offer from _____	Job Offer from _____	Job Offer from _____
Position			
• Title	_____	_____	_____
• Key Responsibilities	_____	_____	_____
Salary			
• Base salary *(annual salary)*	_____	_____	_____
• Commission *(dollar amount or percentage of annual salary and conditions of payment)*	_____	_____	_____
• Bonus *(dollar amount or percentage of annual salary and conditions of payment)*	_____	_____	_____
• Signing Bonus *(dollar amount or percentage of annual salary and conditions of payment)*	_____	_____	_____
• Stock Options *(number of options, option price, and vesting)*	_____	_____	_____
Benefits—Vacation			
• Vacation Days *(number of days and when earned)*	_____	_____	_____
• Personal Holidays *(number of days)*	_____	_____	_____
• Holidays *(number of days)*	_____	_____	_____
• Sick Days *(number of days)*	_____	_____	_____
• Other *(number of days)*	_____	_____	_____
Benefits—Insurance			
• When available after start date	_____	_____	_____
• Medical *(cost per pay period)*	_____	_____	_____
• Dental *(cost per pay period)*	_____	_____	_____
• Optical *(cost per pay period)*	_____	_____	_____
• Life *(cost per pay period)*	_____	_____	_____
• Long-term Disability *(cost per pay period)*	_____	_____	_____
• Short-term Disability *(cost per pay period)*	_____	_____	_____

Continues on the next page...

Compensation Element	Job Offer from _____	Job Offer from _____	Job Offer from _____
Benefits—Other Income/Savings			
• 401(k) Plan *(yes or no; # of waiting days to participate)*	_____ _____	_____ _____	_____ _____
• 401(k) Matching *(percentage of contribution)*	_____	_____	_____
• Other	_____	_____	_____
Benefits—Other			
• Tuition Reimbursement	_____	_____	_____
• Day Care	_____	_____	_____
• Elder Care	_____	_____	_____
• On-site Amenities	_____	_____	_____
• Car Allowance *(dollar amount paid monthly)*	_____	_____	_____
• Relocation	_____	_____	_____
• Other	_____	_____	_____

But Is It the Right Offer for YOU?

Once you have established the monetary value of your offer or offers, it's just as important to evaluate whether this is the offer that's right. Don't take an offer just because it's the only offer you have. You have to go to work every day so you want to be sure that you accept the offer that's right for YOU.

Take a few minutes after you determine the value of your job offer and consider the pros and cons of the offer or offers. It's not always the salary that should be the deciding factor in accepting a job offer. Some other elements in addition to compensation are

- Distance and time of the commute to work
- Option to work remotely
- Work environment
- People with whom and for whom you will work
- Culture of the company
- Dress code (casual vs. formal)
- Employee turnover
- Opportunity for personal development and career advancement
- Job function (is it or will it lead you to what you want to do)
- Social responsibility of the company
- Community involvement of the company
- Reputation of the company

- Stability of the company
- Travel requirements/opportunity
- Relocation requirements/opportunity

Use Activity 16.2 to consider all the elements that are important to you. Keep in mind that any one pro or con can make a job a great fit...or a not-so-great fit. Only **you** can determine that based on what's important to you.

ACTIVITY 16.2 Pros and Cons of Your Job Offer

Instructions: When you get a job offer or offers, complete the following worksheet. Think about all of the elements that are important to you and put them in the appropriate column. You can use this to evaluate one job offer or multiple job offers.

Job	Pros	Cons
Job Offer #1		
Job Offer #2		

Negotiating Offers

Negotiate to Win
Identify one or two key items (such as increased salary, additional vacation days, etc.) that you want and keep your negotiations focused on those. You will be more likely to get want you want if have a targeted approach.

Now that the job has been offered and you've decided you want it, you're ready to negotiate. Keep in mind that you should complete Activities 16.1 and 16.2 after you receive a job offer or offers but before you accept an offer. **You should not officially accept the offer until you have negotiated the offer that you will accept.** If you accept the position before you negotiate, you lose your negotiating power.

About half of all job seekers accept the first offer that's put on the table, but some employers expect candidates to counteroffer. Remember that the employer won't withdraw the offer just because you counter it. So go ahead and ask for what you want—you have nothing to lose and perhaps a lot to gain. Prepare a counteroffer, including salary and benefits. Complete Activity 16.3 Pre-Negotiation Worksheet before you begin negotiating. This will help you identify those items that are most important to you during the negotiation. You probably won't be able to negotiate on every aspect of the offer, so pick the one or two things that are most important to you. Your **pre-negotiation goals** are those things that you consider to be "deal breakers"; if you don't get those, you won't accept the offer. Your **counteroffer** is what you will ask for in each area. Your counteroffer should be for a little more than your pre-negotiation goals in order to allow some room for negotiation.

Also be prepared to review your strengths—the ways you will add value to the firm—as justification for the terms you are seeking. It is also helpful to discuss current market values for this type of position to support your request.

Keep a positive outlook during the negotiation. Settle the issue of salary first and then move into a discussion of benefits. Sometimes with entry-level positions there isn't much room for negotiation of salary, but a signing bonus, an extra week of vacation time, or an early salary review are all items that may sweeten the deal for you.

Some things for which you might consider negotiating:

- Additional vacation time
- Availability of medical insurance at start date (some companies have a 30–90 day waiting period)
- Waiving of one or two months of health care insurance premiums
- Signing bonus
- Performance bonus
- Stock options

Real Fact
Companies reimburse employees for travel expenses relating to company business. If you accept a position that requires out-of-state or local travel, you will be able to submit your receipts for reimbursement. Travel by car is usually reimbursed by the mile according to the company policy or the government rate found at **www.gsa.gov**.

Coordinating Timing of Multiple Offers

Since you are probably interviewing with multiple companies at the same time, it's likely you can expect offers from more than one company. However, not every interviewing process moves at the same pace, so you probably won't get multiple offers at exactly the same time. If this is the case, when you get your first offer (and tell the company you want some time to consider it), it's best to call the other company (or companies) and ask your contact person about the timing for the next steps in the interview process. An example of how you might handle this is

"I wanted to touch base and see if you can give me some insight as to when you will be making your decision (let person respond). I'm very interested in the position and working for your company. I am considering another offer right now and I want to be sure I make my decision with as much information as possible."

It's always best to call the second company so you can get some feedback about timing and if you are still being considered as a candidate. You may not be able to move the process any faster, but you can signal your situation and get some insight before you make your final decision.

Using One Offer to Negotiate Another Offer

What if you have an offer from the first company and want to use it to negotiate an offer from the second company? As mentioned above, it's good to negotiate. But keep in mind that you are negotiating with a future employer, not buying a house. **You want the negotiation to be professional and positive.**

Keep your negotiation focused on exactly what you want from the negotiation and underscoring your value. It's acceptable to mention the fact that you have another offer at a higher salary (or more extensive benefits or more vacation time, etc). But don't disclose the company name, or exact compensation package. Chances are the company will not match an offer just for the sake of matching an offer unless there is a severe shortage of entry-level candidates (remember, you don't have any experience yet). Companies pay what they consider the job to be worth. Your objective is establish your value to get the additional salary, vacation or other benefits that you want.

Negotiating Your Start Date

You may want to take some time off before you start work, your new employer may want you to start right away. **Discuss your start date after you negotiate your salary and benefits.** Your start date is a short-term consideration; your compensation package is a long-term consideration. It's important not to trade off compensation for a later start date.

Pre-Negotiation Worksheet

Instructions: Complete this worksheet after you receive your offer, but before you negotiate the offer. Use the detailed listing in Activity 16.1 to identify areas you would like to increase. The Current Offer is what you have been offered. The Pre-Negotiation Goal is the minimum you must have in order to accept the offer. The Counteroffer is what you will go back to the company and ask for, which should be slightly more than your Pre-Negotiation Goal.

Compensation Element	Current Offer	Pre-Negotiation Goal	Counteroffer
Salary			
Vacation			
Insurance			
Other Income/Savings			
Relocation Benefits			
Other Benefits			

Discuss your intentions with your new employer and come to an agreement as to what date will work best. It's acceptable to start at least two to four weeks after you accept the job. In some industries, such as accounting, you may accept a job offer up to a year in advance. An internship may have a longer or shorter lead time depending on the industry, company, and time of year.

Accepting the Offer

Offer Letter

An offer letter is standard for internships and full-time positions. Be sure you get an offer letter within one to three days of accepting the offer verbally. If you are already working, don't give notice at your current job until you receive your offer letter for your new job.

Once you have agreed to a final offer, you should verbally recap all the elements of the offer. Then you should ask for an offer letter. Every internship and full-time job offer should formally be extended with an offer letter. If the company will not provide an offer letter, don't take the job.

An offer letter is a letter of agreement of the terms of the offer. It usually contains the following as appropriate:

- Title of the position which you are being offered
- Person to whom you will report (optional)

- Location of office (optional)
- Starting salary (either hourly or annual)
- Bonus, commission, signing bonus, car allowance or any additional compensation
- Number of stock options, option price, and vesting schedule
- Vacation days (may reference company benefits package)
- Other benefits (may reference company benefits package)
- Start date
- Any offer contingencies such as passing a company-paid drug screening, background or security check, and/or references

Examples of offer letters are shown here and in Figures 16.1 and 16.2.

Figure 16.1—Offer letter for full-time job

Rich, Talbot and Wells Advertising
1 North Wacker Drive, Suite 3100
Chicago, IL 60600

June 11, 2008

Mr. John Morton
4851 Hudson Avenue
Chicago, IL 60606

Dear John,

We are pleased to extend this offer of employment to you as Account Coordinator reporting to Sarah Welch, Account Director. Your compensation package will include the following:

- Annual salary of $45,000 with performance and salary review on an annual basis.

- Annual performance bonus of 5% of your base salary based upon meeting agreed performance objectives. Your bonus will be prorated for 2008.

- Two weeks of vacation according to the company vacation policy.

- Participation in the 401(k) program upon eligibility outlined in the enclosed *Employee Benefits Package.*

- Participation in the company health plan after 90 days of employment.

- Participation in all other company benefits outlined in the enclosed *Employee Benefits Package.*

Your start date will be July 1, 2008. We are looking forward to you joining our team. If I can be of any further assistance, please don't hesitate to call me.

Sincerely,

Anne Sullivan
Director of Human Resources

Enclosure

Figure 16.2—Offer letter for internship

AJA, Inc. 4545 City Avenue
Philadelphia, PA 19104

May 1, 2008

Ms. Christine Spenser
1102 Main Street
Philadelphia, PA 19191

Dear Christine,

I am pleased to confirm your acceptance of employment as Accounting Intern reporting to Leslie West, Accounting Manager. As agreed, your start date is May 19, 2008. Please report to the Accounting Department located on the 5th floor at 4545 City Avenue at 8:45 a.m.

You will be entitled to all benefits outlined in the attached copy of *A Guide for New Employees*. Your hourly wage will be $16.00.

Our offer of employment is contingent upon your ability to verify that you are lawfully allowed to work in the United States as well as our receipt of satisfactory reference and background checks.

Please accept my personal welcome and well wishes for success in your new position. Welcome to AJA, Inc.

Sincerely,

Pat Ryan
Manager of Recruiting

Attachment

A Personal Touch

After you accept an offer, it's a good idea to send a hand-written thank-you note to everyone with whom you interviewed. It's a nice touch to thank each person for his or her support and tell him or her how excited you are about joining the company. Each person will appreciate your note and you will start off your new job on the right foot.

You should have an offer letter within one to three days of accepting the offer. It is acceptable if the offer letter is sent via e-mail as long as it is on the company letterhead.

When you get your offer letter, review it carefully to be sure it includes all of the elements to which you agreed. If it doesn't, call the author of the letter immediately to get clarification and resolution on the issue. Some companies require you to sign the offer letter and return it to the company. It's best to make a copy of the signed offer letter before you return it. **Keep your offer letter along with all other information from the company in a reference file.**

Congratulations! It's time to enjoy your career. Here's to Brand YOU.

My Career Journal

Name three compensation elements that are most important to you. _____

_____

_____

_____

Name three elements of a job that are important to you but are not part of compensation, such as culture, location, work environment, social responsibility of the company, etc. _____

_____

_____

_____

Thinking about your future job, what is the most important element to you about your job? About the company for which you will work? About the culture of the company? _____

_____

_____

_____

Notes to Myself

Toolkit

Table of Contents

Getting Started—Creating Your Action Plan and Timeline

Every successful marketing campaign starts with a plan. Now it's time to create your work plan. Your work plan will be your road map. And it will be a tool to help you pace your career planning and work search so that you don't feel like you are rushing to get an internship or full-time job at the last minute.

The Best Time to Conduct Your Job Search

When is the best time to start your career planning and work search? It's never too early. **The 5 Steps to Real Success** is a process that is iterative. That means that you can go through the steps many times. Or, you may want to revisit one or two of the steps as you progress through your academic career. The earlier you do your career planning, the better prepared you will be when you want to apply for an internship or a full-time job.

When are companies hiring? It depends. In some areas, such as accounting and finance, internships and full-time jobs are usually filled in the fall with starting dates in the spring. Generally, this is also true for large companies that have a structured internship or training program. However, advertising agencies, PR agencies, event planning companies, and other professional services providers are usually hiring all year since their staffing needs are dependent on when they acquire new clients.

Keep in mind that there is even more competition for internships and full-time jobs at the end of the school year. You want to get your cover letter and resumé out early to avoid getting lost in the crowd.

General Timeline and Action Plan

The best way to get something done is to put your plan on paper. Now that you have identified some areas that you are interested in pursuing, it's time to create your work plan.

Following is a general timeline for **The 5 Steps to Real Success**. This timeline is designed to complete the steps in a time frame as short as a semester or as long as 6 months. In the blank Action Plan and Timeline on the next page, you will be able to create your own Action Plan and Timeline and adjust the time frames so they work for your schedule.

General Timeline—The 5 Steps to Real Success

Step	Approximate Time to Complete	Notes
Step 1—Choosing Your Path • Read Chapters 1–3. • Complete activities in Chapters 1–3.	3 weeks	It's best to complete this step as soon as possible so you can begin thinking and gathering information to choose your path. You may want to revisit these chapters later in your academic career and reevaluate or refine your path.
Step 2—Researching the Market • Read Chapters 4–7. • Complete activities in Chapters 4–7.	4–6 weeks	Do extensive research on the market, your target industries, and target companies. You will use this research in Step 4—Communicating Your Value Proposition.
Step 3—Creating Your Value Proposition • Read Chapters 8–11. • Complete activities in Chapters 8–11.	4–6 weeks	This is where you actually start crafting Brand You. The activities will help you create the framework for your resumé and cover letter.
Step 4—Communicating Your Value Proposition • Read Chapters 12–14. • Complete activities in Chapters 12–14. • Create your resumé. • Write at least one cover letter directed to your target audience. • Send out your cover letter and resumé using as many "media" as possible.	3–6 weeks	This is the step where Brand You comes alive for your "customers"—prospective employers. You will want to use every method to get your cover letter and resumé to as many people as possible in your target audience. "Advertise" as much as possible and let prospective employers know about "you."
Step 5—Delivering Your Value Proposition • Read Chapters 15–16. • Complete activities in Chapters 15–16. • Reread Chapter 15 prior to each interview.	2–8 weeks	This is your opportunity to impress your prospective employer and learn if the company and position is what you want. Don't just grab the first job that's offered. If you get out enough cover letters and resumés, you will have plenty of job offers. Be sure you evaluate your offers completely and ask the right questions.

Creating Your Personal Action Plan and Timeline

It's time for you to create your own work plan, including your action plan and timeline. You may adjust it based on changes in your schedule, but it's best to create your work plan and revise it as needed.

Organization is key for your work search. Keep your work plan easily accessible so you can stay on track. You may want to set up task reminders so you don't lose track of the steps you want to complete by your due dates.

*Instructions: Fill in your Estimated Start Dates and Estimated Completion Dates for each of **The 5 Steps to Real Success** based on your schedule. Stay organized and review this work plan weekly. Update your Actual Start Dates and Actual Completion Dates so you can stay on your schedule.*

My Work Plan and Timeline

Date of Work Plan _____

Action Plan	Estimated Start Date	Estimated Completion Date	Actual Start Date	Actual Completion Date	Notes
Step 1—Choosing Your Path					
• Read Chapters 1–3.	_____	_____	_____	_____	_____
• Complete activities in Chapters 1–3.	_____	_____	_____	_____	_____
Step 2—Researching the Market					
• Read Chapters 4–7.	_____	_____	_____	_____	_____
• Complete activities in Chapters 4–7.	_____	_____	_____	_____	_____
Step 3—Creating Your Value Proposition					
• Read Chapters 8–11.					
• Complete activities in Chapters 8–11.	_____	_____	_____	_____	_____
• Create your resumé.	_____	_____	_____	_____	_____
• Write at least three versions of your cover letter directed at different target audiences.	_____	_____	_____	_____	_____

Continued on the next page...

My Work Plan and Timeline

Date of Work Plan _____

Action Plan	Estimated Start Date	Estimated Completion Date	Actual Start Date	Actual Completion Date	Notes
Step 4—Communicating Your Value Proposition					
• Read Chapters 12–14.	_____	_____	_____	_____	_____
• Complete activities in Chapters 12–14.	_____	_____	_____	_____	_____
• **On-line**. Complete a list of target Web sites including job boards, professional organizations, and at least 25 companies.	_____	_____	_____	_____	_____
• **On-line**. Set up e-mail alerts on job boards, professional organization and target company Web sites.	_____	_____	_____	_____	_____
• **On-line**. Review existing personal social networking pages to ensure all content is appropriate.	_____	_____	_____	_____	_____
• **On-line**. Join professional social networking Web sites.	_____	_____	_____	_____	_____
• **On-line**. Create professional Web site including resumé and work samples.	_____	_____	_____	_____	_____
• **Direct Mail**. Conduct research on target companies to identify names, titles, and addresses of people in companies to whom you want to send your cover letter and resumé. Create your mailing lists in Microsoft Word or Excel.	_____	_____	_____	_____	_____
• **Direct Mail**. Purchase mailing supplies.	_____	_____	_____	_____	_____

Continued on the next page...

My Work Plan and Timeline

Date of Work Plan _____

Action Plan	Estimated Start Date	Estimated Completion Date	Actual Start Date	Actual Completion Date	Notes
• **Direct Mail**. Complete mail merge and mail letters.	_____	_____	_____	_____	
• **Career Fairs**. Research dates and locations of upcoming Career Fairs.	_____	_____	_____	_____	
• **Career Fairs**. Complete a Career Fair Action Plan (Activity 12.4) for each fair.	_____	_____	_____	_____	
• **Follow-up**. Add follow-up columns to mailing lists. Set dates for follow-up.	_____	_____	_____	_____	
• **Follow-up**. Monitor follow-up dates daily and call, write, or e-mail as appropriate.	_____	_____	_____	_____	
Step 5—Delivering Your Value Proposition					
• Read Chapters 15 and 16.	_____	_____	_____	_____	
• Complete activities in Chapters 15 and 16 (as appropriate).	_____	_____	_____	_____	
• Reread Chapters 15 and 16 prior to each interview.	_____	_____	_____	_____	
• Enjoy your new job!	_____	_____	_____	_____	

Recommended Web Sites

Review these Web sites and descriptions. Visit those that you think will help you target your job search. Use this list as a reference when you complete Activity 12.1. Don't forget to include Web sites for local professional organizations (such as the local advertising club) and local job boards.

Web Site Type	URL	Description
Career Planning	www.rileyguide.com	Comprehensive career site with links for researching careers and jobs in all disciplines and international jobs
Career Planning	www.bls.gov/OCO	Occupational Outlook Handbook from the U. S. Department of Labor
Career Planning	www.salary.com	Salaries for varies jobs; compares salaries in various cities; includes links to www.careerbuilder.com
Career Planning, Job Board, and More	Usually listed on your school Web site	Your campus career center, library, and alumni organization are excellent resources
Career Planning and Job Board	www.experience.com	Articles, tips, blogs with career planning insights including section for internships; includes job board
Career Planning and Job Board	www.collegegrad.com	Career information geared to college students; includes job board
Career Planning and Job Board	www.wetfeet.com	Career planning information and job board; includes job board
Career Planning and Job Board	www.career-advice. monster.com/	Career planning and job search articles; also includes one of the largest job boards on the Internet www. monster.com
Career Planning and Job Board	www.job-hunt.org	Career planning information, links to other Web sites and job board
Career Planning and Job Board	www.careerbuilder.com	Career planning articles and one of the largest job boards on the Internet
Career Planning and Job Board	www.jobweb.com	Web site of the National Association of Colleges and Employers; career planning articles and tips; links to college career center Web sites
Career Planning and Job Board	www.black-collegian.com	Career information, news, and job board with a focus on African Americans
Career Planning and Job Board	www.hispanicbusiness.com	Information about Hispanic businesses with link to www.hirediversity.com job board
Career Planning and Job Board	www.vault.com	Information and articles on career planning, salaries and, more including internships; includes job board
Career Planning and Job Board	www.online.wsj.com/public/ page/news-career-jobs.html	Career site from the *Wall Street Journal*
Job Board	www.aftercollege.com	Job board focused on internships and entry-level jobs

Continued on the next page...

Web Site Type	URL	Description
Job Board	www.craigslist.com	One of the largest job boards on the Internet
Job Board	www.hotjobs.yahoo.com	Large job board; also includes articles on conducting a job search
Job Board	www.nationjob.com	Large job board for jobs of all kinds
Job Board	www.monstertrak.com	Large job board with focus on internships and entry-level jobs
Job Search Engine	www.indeed.com	An aggregator of job listings; search by key word and location
Job Search Engine	www.internshipprograms.com	Search engine for internships
Job Search Engine	www.internweb.com	Search engine for internships
Professional Networking	www.linkedin.com	Largest professional social network on the Internet
Professional Networking	www.ryze.com	Professional social network
Professional Networking	www.jobster.com	Professional social network
Professional Networking	www.ziggs.com	Professional social network
Professional Association Job Board	www.associationjobboards.com	Links to Web sites of professional associations and job boards
Accounting and Finance	www.afponline.org	Web site for Association for Financial Professionals; includes job board
Accounting and Finance	www.fpanet.org	Web site for the Financial Planning Association; includes job board
Accounting and Finance	www.accountingjobstoday.com	Job board specializing in accounting jobs
Accounting and Finance	www.garp.com	Web site for Global Association of Risk Professionals; includes job board
Accounting and Finance	www.aicpa.org	Web site of the American Institute of Certified Public Accountants; includes job board
Accounting and Finance	www.theiia.org	Web site for the Institute of Internal Auditors; includes job board
Accounting and Finance	www.jobsinthemoney.com	Job board specializing in accounting and finance jobs
Accounting and Finance	www.accounting.com	Job board specializing in accounting jobs
Accounting and Finance	www.bankjobs.com	Job board specializing in accounting and finance jobs
Advertising	www.aaaa.org	Web site of the American Association of Advertising Agencies; includes job board
Advertising	www.aaf.org	Web site of the American Advertising Federation; includes a job board
Advertising	www.redbooks.com	Directory of advertising agencies and key management members
Entrepreneur	www.inc.com	Web site of *Inc.* magazine; information, articles, and resources for entrepreneurs
Entrepreneur	www.entrepreneur.com	Web site with business ideas, opportunities, tools, and services for entrepreneurs

Continued on the next page...

Web Site Type	URL	Description
Entrepreneur	www.score.org	Web site for SCORE, Counselors to America's Small Businesses and partner with Small Business Association (SBA); free business counseling available
Event Planning	www.bizbash.com	Event planning organization; excellent free magazine
Freelance/Independent Contractor	www.ifreelance.com	Job board for freelancer service providers and open projects
Freelance/Independent Contractor	www.sologig.com	Consulting, contract, temporary, or freelance opportunities
International	www.internationaljobs.org	Job board for international jobs
International	www.ihipo.com	Social network based in Singapore; includes job board
International	www.monster.com/geo/siteselection.asp	International portion of Monster.com; search jobs by country
Internet Marketing	www.sempo.org	Web site of Search Engine Marketing Professional Organization; includes job board
Internet Marketing	www.marketingsherpa.com	On-line marketing articles and job board
Internet Marketing	www.shop.org	Web site of the National Retail Federation; includes job board
Internet Marketing	www.webanalyticsassociation.org	Web site of the Web Analytics Association; includes job board
Internet Marketing	www.iab.net	Web site of the Internet Advertising Bureau focused on the continued growth of interactive advertising
Management	www.amanet.org	Web site of the American Management Association; includes job board
Management	www.shrm.org	Web site of Society for Human Resource Management; includes job board
Marketing	www.the-dma.org	Web site of the Direct Marketing Association; includes a job board
Marketing	www.fmi.org	Web site of the Food Marketing Institute
Marketing	www.stylecareers.com	Job board for fashion, apparel, and retail jobs
Marketing	www.marketingjobs.com	Job board for jobs in marketing
Marketing	www.marketinghire.com	Job board for jobs in marketing
Marketing	www.talentzoo.com	Job board for jobs in marketing, advertising, and PR
Marketing Research	www.mra-net.org	Web site of the Marketing Research Association
Public Relations	www.prsa.org	Web site of the Public Relations Society of America; includes job board
Public Relations	www.prssa.org	Public Relations Student Society of America; includes job board
Public Relations and Communications	www.iabc.com	Web site of the International Association of Business Communicators; includes job board
Sales and Marketing	www.smei.org	Web site of Sales and Marketing Executives International; includes job board

Do's and Don'ts of On-line Job Searching

Whether you are submitting your cover letter and resumé on-line, via e-mail, or posting your professional profile or video resumé to a professional social network Web site, there are mistakes that could cost you the opportunity for an interview. Be savvy on-line by following the Do's and Don'ts.

Here Are the Practices You Should DO:

- **DO:** Spell check and proof every communication you send or post. That includes cover letter, resumé, professional profile and every e-mail you send. One typo or grammatical error can eliminate you from consideration for an interview. Ask someone (a professor, a parent, or someone in the business world) to proof your resumé and cover letter before you post them or send them out.

- **DO:** Submit your cover letter and resumé in PDF format when applying for jobs through an on-line job board as it will maintain the formatting. Go to **www.acrobat.com** and click on Create PDF and follow the prompts. Review the PDF documents to be sure page breaks are correct.

- **DO:** Also save a copy of your cover letter and resumé in Microsoft Word as most companies require this format. If you are using Word 2007, save the documents as Word 97–2003 documents so all recipients can open them. Also save a copy of your cover letter and resumé as a plain text file using Microsoft Word. Be sure to fix any line breaks or odd characters before you save it. If a job board does not accept a PDF, submit your resumé as a plain text document. This will make it easier for employers to read.

- **DO:** Do use your cover letter as the body of the e-mail when you are sending your resumé to someone via e-mail. Modify and personalize the letter to make it appropriate to the addressee and attach your resumé as a Word document. Your cover letter highlights your value proposition so the addressee can see at a glance (and without an extra click) what makes you unique. A short e-mail is **not** enough, even if you are sending your resumé to someone you know. Chances are the person to whom you are sending your e-mail is going to forward your e-mail to someone else. Stand out by using your e-mail to sell your brand.

- **DO:** Review the privacy policy of job boards and Web sites before you post your resumé. Based on the privacy policy, you may want to consider applying for specific jobs rather than posting your resumé to minimize your exposure for identity theft and getting unwanted e-mail solicitations.

- **DO:** Identify key words to search for jobs on job boards and other Web site job listings. The right key words increase your chances of seeing relevant jobs.

- **DO:** Incorporate your key words into your cover letter and resumé so that when companies put your information into their databases, you increase your chances of your resumé being included in the search results. Need help identifying key words? Stop by the library and get some ideas from the librarian or stop by the campus career center and ask for ideas.

- **DO:** Include the job code from the Web posting in the subject line of the e-mail when applying for a job. Be sure to also mention the job title for which you are applying in your cover letter.

- **DO:** Join professional social networks such as **www.linkedin.com** and create a profile, start a professional network, and ask for introductions to other people in your target industry, and search for jobs.

- **DO:** Create a professional Web site including your resumé and samples of your work. Include writing samples, projects, papers and presentations from your internships, volunteer work or major classes, and other business-related content. Be sure this is all your work and does not violate any copyright or privacy issues. This Web site serves as your on-line branding statement. You should limit the amount of personal information (such as address and phone number) to minimize the risk of identity theft.

- **DO:** Search your name on all major search engines such as Google, Yahoo, AOL, and Ask. The search results are those that your prospective employers will see. Be sure all pages are consistent with your brand message.

- **DO:** Set up a Google News alert, **www.news.google.com**, for all target companies and any companies with whom you may be interviewing. You will get an e-mail about any breaking news as it happens so you will be informed about company news for an interview.

- **DO:** Send thank-you notes within 24 hours to everyone with whom you interview. An e-mail thank you is very acceptable; a hand-written note is especially effective.

Here Are the Practices That Are DON'Ts:

- **DON'T:** Include pictures, videos, blogs, or other entries on your social networking pages or other Web sites that are not appropriate for a prospective employer to see. You are marketing your personal brand 24/7 so edit your pages accordingly. (That means removing the spring break video from YouTube.)

- **DON'T:** Use abbreviations or text messaging language in business communications, even if you know the person with whom you are communicating. Keep your communications professional.

- **DON'T:** Send your cover letter and resumé to your target companies via e-mail. Since the addressee doesn't know you, your resumé will most likely be deleted or treated as spam. Also, don't use services to e-mail blast your resumé to companies or recruiters. Direct mail is a more effective way to contact people in companies that are on your target list. And, your paper cover letter and resumé will stand out in the sea of daily e-mails.

- **DON'T:** Save documents such as your resumé and cover letter with file names other than your name and type of document. For example, a file name for a resumé such as "official version" is not appropriate to submit to a job posting. Make it easy for a prospective employer and reflect professionalism by saving your resumé and cover letter documents with file names such as "Michael Bayers resumé" and "Michael Bayers cover letter."

- **DON'T:** Use a personal e-mail address that isn't professional for business communications. If your current personal e-mail address is something like partygirl@comcast.net, set up a new e-mail account with Gmail, Hotmail, or other internet service provider. Use the new e-mail address or your college or university e-mail address on your resumé.

- **DON'T:** Use a video resumé just because it is a novel use of technology. A video resumé should be used only to supplement a traditional resumé and cover letter. Only use one if you are extremely comfortable in front of the camera and you can produce the video professionally. Also, keep in mind that some companies won't use video resumés due to potential discrimination issues (e.g., hiring someone based on appearance rather than skills).

- **DON'T:** Leave electronic devices turned on during an interview. Turn off your cell phone or PDA (don't just put it on vibrate) and put it out of sight before you go into the building for the interview. Leave your iPod, PSP, or any other electronic devices at home. Demonstrate that the interview is the most important thing to you by not having any disruptions.

- **DON'T:** Forget that the on-line world meets the real world. Use courtesy, professionalism, and a personal touch in every communication.

Internships 101: What You Should Know about an Internship

Why an Internship?

One word says it all—experience.

If you have an internship on your resumé, you have an advantage over students who don't have an internship. An internship allows you to stand out, be different, offer value, get experience, impress a prospective employer, add to your personal network, and get the job you want. Don't underestimate the power of an internship on your resumé.

Where Is the Best Place to Look for an Internship?

Follow **The 5 Steps to Real Success** in *Brand You*. The process is the same for internships and full-time jobs. Chapter 4—Career Information and Research and Recommended Web Sites in the *Brand You* Toolkit are excellent sources to help you conduct research and identify internship opportunities.

When Is the Best Time to Look for an Internship?

Timing depends on the industry and company. Fall is the best time to apply for spring and summer internships at companies that have structured internship programs. Many company Web sites list cut-off dates for internship applications. For some industries, including many advertising agencies, public relations agencies, interactive marketing agencies, and other professional services providers, internships are usually created based on need and timing depends on when new clients come onboard. These companies hire all year round. Read the business journals and trade publications to see who recently won a new account. Chances are they will be looking to ramp up fast.

The bottom line is it's never too early and it's never a bad time to start investigating and applying for internships.

Paid vs. Unpaid Internship—Which Is Better?

You might think the obvious answer is that a paid internship is better than an unpaid internship. But that's not always the case. What's important is to get experience in the industry you think you want to pursue. In some industries, an internship is a requirement in order to be considered for a full-time job. If you can find a paid internship that will give you the experience you want, take it. But don't be short-sighted when you search for an internship. If you can afford to give up the income, choose your internship based on what experience you will get. You'll find it will pay you back when you look for a full-time job.

Test Drive Your Career Choice

An internship is great experience and it can lead to a full-time job in the same company or industry. But an internship is also a great way to find out what you DON'T want to do. You may not like your internship. You may want to change your career path as a result of an internship. That's great news because you can focus your efforts on another industry or specialty that you might like better. And, you still get the benefit of having experience on your resumé. So go ahead, test drive your career choice with an internship.

An Internship Is What You Make It

Just because you get an internship doesn't mean you've arrived. An internship can include a lot of repetitive and sometimes boring tasks. And, it also can include stimulating and thought-provoking assignments including exposure to senior management and clients, challenging projects, inclusion in major meetings, and more.

When you land an internship, get involved. Sometimes managers are too busy to spend the time to train interns. If that's the case, train yourself. Ask questions of co-workers, read as much information as you can, learn the company systems, get involved in anything that's going on in your department, volunteer to work on projects even if they are boring, work overtime when needed, walk through the office with your head high and introduce yourself to anyone you pass; make people remember you. Think of your internship as a 10-week job interview. Just like an interview, an internship is what you make it.

Sample Resumés and Cover Letters

Sample Resumé for Jessica Freeman

Jessica Freeman
8724 Ninth Avenue
Oak Park, IL 60301
Phone: 312-555-1212 E-mail: jfreeman123@gmail.com
www.jessicafreeman.com

Profile	• Creative problem solver with a strong work ethic. • Highly organized with ability to manage multiple priorities. • Experience at advertising agency; involved in community service organizations.
Education	City State University, Chicago, IL Bachelor of Science, Marketing 2008
Scholarships and Awards	Dean's List 2007, 2008 2008 Loyola Scholarship Award
Internship May-Aug 2007	**The Solomon Group, Chicago, IL** Intern, Client Services • Collaborated with the client services team that worked on the repositioning of Noah's Dairy Products. • Created and sent weekly customer e-mails to 300,000 customers. • Maintained customer e-mail segmentation lists using Blue Hornet e-mail tool. • Monitored paid search budget and ROI by key word in Google Ad Words; identified 50 new key words that generated an additional 8% in revenue. • Prepared weekly and monthly paid search reports that were used by the senior management team using Omniture web analytics tool. • Assisted in analysis of consumer purchase patterns and report that was presented to the client. • Participated in client and vendor meetings. • Maintained client conference reports.
Work Experience Summer 2005–6	**The Federal Reserve Bank, Chicago, IL** Currency Sorter • Reviewed $150,000 of dollar bills daily and determine which will be destroyed and which will be recycled; team leader of the student section.
Summer 2004	**Macy's, Chicago, IL** Sales Associate • Served customers and resolved customer service issues in the Junior Department; completed Selling Stars sales training.
Activities	Coats for Kids – Marketing Coordinator • Raised contributions for $25,000 in new coats for 500 children. Alpha Phil Sorority – Secretary • Raised $3,000 for American Heart Association.
Skills	Microsoft Word, PowerPoint, Excel, Outlook, Adobe Acrobat, Google Ad Words, Blue Hornet E-mail Tool, Omniture Web Analytics Tool

Sample Resumé for Jonathan Vitale

Jonathan Vitale

541 North Elm Street Dayton, OH 12345

615-333-5555   jvitale@brookstonecollege.edu

www.jonathanvitale.com

Objective

To obtain an internship position at an agency or company with focus on interactive marketing and new media.

Education

Brookstone College, Boston, MA

Bachelor of Science in Marketing, expected May 2009

Marketing Experience

2005 to present

American Marketing Association, Boston, MA

Student Member

- Created a social networking strategy to increase student membership of the American Marketing Association on campus.
- Organized five student events sponsored by the American Marketing Association; increased student attendance by 22% compared to last year.
- Designed and implemented an ongoing student e-mail campaign; increased e-mail database by 12%.
- Developed and launched Facebook and MySpace pages for the student American Marketing Association.
- Increased student membership by 17%.

2006 to present

Boston Advertising Club, Boston, MA

Student Member

- Wrote a weekly blog for the Boston Advertising Club Web site.
- Researched and contributed to regular articles in the Boston Advertising Club bi-monthly magazine.
- Updated the Boston Advertising Club website regularly with events, news, and job postings.
- Maintained member e-mail list.
- Sent out monthly member e-mail newsletters.
- Participated in the annual Addy Awards ceremony.

Work Experience

Summer 2006–7

Janis Construction Company, Dayton, OH

Construction Worker

- Worked on new home construction sites; learned electrical and carpentry skills.

Activities

Saint Katherine of Siena, Dayton, OH

Youth Group, Student Chairperson – Event Committee

- Organized eight fundraising events in 2007–8.
- Raised money to support over 300 local families in need.

Dayton Run for the Cure, Dayton, OH

- Ran in 5K race and raised $800 in sponsorships.

Sample Cover Letter for Jessica Freeman

Jessica Freeman
8724 Ninth Avenue
Oak Park, IL 60301

March 17, 2008

Ms. Diane Phillips
Director of Marketing
Advance Insurance Group
421 Corporate Drive; Suite 300
Chicago, IL 60606

Dear Ms. Phillips,

Can Advance Insurance benefit from an innovative and hard-working Marketing Specialist?

I am currently a senior at City State University and will be graduating in May with a Bachelor of Science degree in Marketing. I believe my educational achievements coupled with my intellectual curiosity and personal energy can bring a fresh perspective to your Marketing Department. Some highlights about my background are as follows:

- **Marketing Experience** – As a Marketing Intern at the Solomon Group, I was a member of the client team that repositioned Noah's Dairy Products. The initiative included developing a new positioning statement, media strategy, and creative strategy. I am also fluent with internet search tools including Google Ad Words, Blue Hornet e-mail tool, and Omniture Web analytics tool.

- **Academic Excellence** – I have been named to the Dean's List for the past 2 years. In addition, I am a recipient of the 2008 Loyola Scholarship Award, which recognizes outstanding academic performance and community service.

- **Community Service** – I am the Marketing Coordinator of Coats for Kids, a non-profit organization that provides coats to elementary schools. In 2008, we donated a record $25,000 worth of new coats to over 500 children in the Chicago metropolitan area.

I would like the opportunity to show you some samples of my work, which include marketing strategy, market research, sales promotion, and advertising. I'll call you the week of March 24 so we can set up a meeting time that is convenient for you. You can reach me at 312-555-1212 or jfreeman123@gmail.com. I look forward to discussing this marketing opportunity.

Sincerely,

Jessica Freeman

Attachment

Sample Cover Letter for Jonathan Vitale

Jonathan Vitale
541 North Elm Street
Dayton, OH 12345

April 21, 2008

Mr. Michael Woods
Account Director
Lane Interactive Advertising
4040 Century Boulevard; Suite 1501
Boston, MA 03456

Dear Mr. Woods,

Congratulations on landing the Dominos Pizza account. I'm sure it's an exciting time at the agency. If you are looking for a motivated individual with a passion for the Internet on your team, I am that person.

I am currently a junior at Brookstone College pursuing a major in Marketing with a focus on Interactive Marketing. I'd like to bring my energy and internet savvy to Lane Interactive Advertising for a summer internship position on one of your client service teams. Some highlights of my background are as follows:

- **Passion for the Internet** – I thrive on the fact that the Internet is continuously evolving and providing new and untapped opportunities for brands. I want to play a role in building brands on-line. As an experienced Internet and technology user, I have the experience and insight to understand how current interactive marketing works and ideas as to how it might work even better.

- **Marketing Trade Group Involvement** – I have gained exposure to the interactive advertising industry as a member of the local chapter of the American Marketing Association and a student member of the Boston Advertising Club.

- **Leadership Experience** – As the Student Chairperson of the Event Committee for the Saint Katherine's Youth Group, I have organized over 8 fund-raising events. As a result of the increased fund-raising, our group was able to provide financial assistance and personal support to over 300 local families in need.

With Dominos as a new client, you need only the best people to support the brand. I am focused and willing to work hard in order to learn the business. I would like the opportunity to show you some examples of my work. I can be reached at 615-333-5555 or via e-mail at jvitale@brookstonecollege.edu. I will touch base the week of April 28 to see what day will be most convenient for you. I look forward to discussing your new challenges.

Sincerely,

Jonathan Vitale

Attachment

Interview Checklist: Be Ready for Every Interview

Review this list before each interview. If you follow these steps, you'll increase your chances of getting the job offer you want!

Before the Interview

- Research the company so you can relate your skills and experience to its products or services. Review the company Web site, go to any stores or retail locations, use their product or service, if possible. Read articles about the company by searching at **www.google.com**, **www.hoovers.com**, **www.bizjournals.com** or the local newspaper Web site.

- Set up a Google News alert (**www.news.google.com**) so you can get any breaking news about the company. Also, news can be important when you are doing your follow-up. It's a great way to let the interviewer know you are current about what's going on with the company. And, if it's news about a new client, new office, increased sales or earnings, you can use that as a reason to follow-up.

- Ask for a job description, if available.

- Analyze the job description and the information you gathered about the company. If you were doing the hiring, what skills, attitudes, and characteristics would you be looking for?

- Complete a NAB (Need, Action, Benefit) worksheet for the position. Develop memorable stories that describe your accomplishments and the benefits.

- Practice your answers to questions out loud. If you've ever given a speech, you know there can be a big difference between what your brain thinks and what your mouth says.

- Develop questions you will ask. Bring them with you in a professional folder or portfolio.

- Print at least three extra copies of your resumé on 24-lb. paper and put them in your folder or portfolio. Even though the interviewer has a copy, it might not be handy at the time of the interview. Also, you may be asked to meet someone who was not originally on the interview schedule. It's always best to be prepared.

- Look up directions to the location of the interview. If possible, do a dry run to be sure of the transportation time including parking, public transit, etc. Be sure you know exactly which building and floor you will be visiting, as well as the name of the person with whom you are meeting.

- Dress professionally. You only have one chance to make a good first impression. If the workplace is casual, dress one step above. It's best to wear business attire. Don't display body piercings or tattoos.
- Plan to arrive early. This allows you time to relax (try deep breathing) and to review the information you want to emphasize. Stop in the restroom and do one last check to be sure you look your best. Have a mint and smile!

During the Interview

- Greet the interviewer with a smile and a firm handshake.
- Make eye contact and smile. This will actually help you relax and enjoy the interview.
- Express a positive attitude and show enthusiasm in your responses.
- Consider the interview a 50/50 exchange—evaluate how well the company fits you.
- Ask good questions.
- Ask about the next steps in the process.
- Ask for the job!

After the Interview

- Send a thank-you note to each person with whom you interviewed within 24 hours. Refer to something specific that you discussed in the interview so the person can connect your note with you. Reiterate your interest in the job. See sample thank-you notes later in the *Brand You* Toolkit.
- Call the interviewer one week after the interview to check on progress. It shows your interest, and it's better to know where you stand than to keep wondering.

Sample Thank-You Note to Interviewer

Dear Diane,

I wanted to say thank you for taking the time to meet with me today. I thoroughly enjoyed our conversation. I was especially excited to hear about the new initiative to reposition Advance Insurance Group. It sounds like there is a lot of work and reward ahead.

My experience at the Solomon Group working on repositioning brands sounds like a perfect fit for the Marketing Specialist position. Based on our meeting, I already have some ideas about how I can add value to your team.

Thank you again for your time and insight. I look forward to the next steps in the interview process.

Sincerely,
Jessica Freeman

Sample Thank-You Note to HR/Recruiter

Dear Jason,

I wanted to send you a note to thank you for arranging all the logistics for my interviews today. I realize that it's not easy to coordinate everyone's schedule, but you did it with ease and good humor.

My meetings with Diane Phillips, John Kisko, Lou Hernandez, and Ty Rowen were interesting and informative. I learned so much about the company and the plans for the future. And even though I didn't get a chance to meet you in person, I feel like I already know you. You are an excellent ambassador for Advance Insurance Group and a true professional.

Thanks again.

Sincerely,
Jessica Freeman

Sample Thank-You Note to Someone Who Provides a Professional Reference

Dear Lee,

Thank you so much for agreeing to provide a reference for me.

I'm very excited about the potential of being offered the position of Marketing Specialist at Advance Insurance Group. After doing my research and going through the interview process, I believe I could bring a lot to the company. And, I think it would be a great environment for me to get my first full-time job in marketing. I'll keep you posted on the outcome of the interview.

A copy of my current resumé is attached for your reference.

Thanks again. I really appreciate and value your support.

Best regards,
Jessica Freeman

FAQs – Frequently Asked Questions about Career Planning and Work Search

If you think you are the only one who has questions about planning your future, your career, and getting a job, think again! Many of the same questions you are asking are the same ones other students are also asking. You will find the most frequently asked questions below along with the page number and chapter reference in *Brand You* where you can find the answers. The questions are organized to follow the flow of **The 5 Steps to Real Success**.

Step 1—Choosing Your Path

Q. I don't even know what my major will be; shouldn't I wait until I choose my major before I use *Brand You*?

A. It's never too early to start planning your future. *Brand You* can help you identify areas in which you have interest and skills. It can help you decide on your major and a direction for your future. It's never too early to start understanding the process of career planning. Read Chapters 1–3 in *Brand You* to see how **The 5 Steps to Real Success** can help you make some important life choices.

Q. I'm only a sophomore. Do I really need to make a choice now about what I'm going to do after I graduate?

A. You don't have to make a commitment now about what you are going to do in the future. But you do need to learn more about what is available, what is most interesting to you and how you can go about getting an internship and ultimately the full-time job you want. Start on page 16 of *Brand You* and see how planning your future now can help you later.

Q. I'm an accounting major. I'm not going to look for a job in marketing, so why would I use *Brand You*?

A. Branding isn't just for marketing majors. Branding is the approach of identifying and communicating your unique talents and skills so that you can set yourself apart from the other candidates and land the internship or full-time job you want. And *Brand You* contains activities and resource information that will help you in your job search, no matter what career path you are pursuing. Start by reading pages 2–7, and don't stop there.

Q. Will I ever find a job I really like?

A. Yes! When you identify the type of environment, industry, and company that best fits you, you will be surprised at how much you will enjoy working. Check out Chapter 3 to see how *Brand You* can help you identify your direction.

Step 2—Researching the Market

Q. I think I'm interested in more than one industry. Do I have to choose just one?

A. You are not restricted to choosing only one industry. You may want to pursue a career in a few different industries. The research, interviewing, and internship process can help you get a better understanding of the direction you want to take. Don't limit yourself. Do your research and pursue the areas that interest you. Chapters 4, 5, and 7 in *Brand You* will help give you some ideas as to how you can approach multiple targets.

Q. Where do I find information about companies that are good to work for?

A. Chapter 4 provides invaluable information about how to research industries and identify companies that might be a good fit for you.

Q. What if I choose an industry now that I think I want to work in, and then change my mind next year?

A. You can't make a mistake. You may choose one or two industries now and change your mind before you graduate. Or, you can change your mind after an internship or even after you start working. Read Chapter 5, especially page 67, to understand that your decisions will guide you and your experience will serve you well.

Step 3—Creating Your Value Proposition

Q. I don't have any experience, what can I put on my resumé?

A. Putting together your resumé takes thought and research. Take the time to read Chapter 8 in *Brand You* to see how you can identify your personal brand's features, benefits, and extras that can become the foundation for your resumé.

Q. Where do I start looking for an internship?

A. Chapter 9 and Internships 101 in the Toolkit in *Brand You* are good places to start. You can get some ideas about how to approach your search for an internship. Don't forget, you'll need a resumé and cover letter so be sure to read all of *Brand You* to understand how you can get the internship you want.

Q. I'm not sure I want to work for a traditional company. What if I want to start my own company or work on my own?

A. There are many, many opportunities outside the corporate world. Read Chapter 10 in *Brand You* to explore some alternatives to a corporate job. You will also find some good Web sites that can provide information and resources to help you discover some appealing options.

Q. How much can I expect to get paid for an internship or full-time job?

A. The best way to determine how much you can expect to get paid is to read Chapter 11 in *Brand You*. This will help you determine how you establish how much you are worth. When you get an offer, be sure to read Chapter 16 so you can evaluate, negotiate, and accept the offer appropriately.

   If you are looking for an internship, keep in mind that not every internship is a paid internship. And, some of the best internships are not paid. Read Internships 101 in the *Brand You* Toolkit to find out what factors to consider when you are pursuing an internship.

Step 4—Communicating Your Value Proposition

Q. What's the right format for a resumé?

A. There is no single format that is right or wrong when it comes to a resumé. However, there are some guidelines and tips in Chapter 13 of *Brand You* that can help make your resumé stand out. Don't forget, your resumé should never travel without your cover letter. Chapter 13 of *Brand You* also includes how to write a powerful cover letter.

Q. How should I get my resumé and cover letter to prospective employers?

A. You have the benefit of using a combination of on-line and traditional methods to let your target employers know that you are in the market for an internship or a full-time job. Read Chapter 12 in *Brand You* and put together an integrated marketing communications plan for your brand. And, the Do's and Don'ts of On-line Job Searching in the *Brand You* Toolkit is also helpful to avoid the pitfalls of using the internet for your job search.

Q. Everyone says that most jobs are filled by networking, but I don't have a network. What else can I do?

A. You'll be surprised at how many people you know when you read Chapter 14 in *Brand You* and learn how to master your networking skills.

Step 5—Delivering Your Value Proposition

Q. How do I prepare for an interview?

A. An interview is an opportunity for the company to learn about you and for you to learn about the company whether you are interviewing for an internship or a full-time job. But you only have one chance to make a good first impression, so read Chapter 15 in *Brand You* before every interview to be ready to impress.

Q. What if I'm interviewing at two companies and get an offer from one of them. How can I get an offer from the other company before I accept the first offer?

A. It's perfectly acceptable to ask for some time to consider an offer before you accept it. Find out how to handle this situation in Chapter 16 of *Brand You*.

Q. What's the best way to negotiate an offer?

A. Salary is not the only element of compensation. Read Chapter 16 to understand other benefits that can be a part of your negotiation.

Epilogue

This is not the end of the book. It is actually the first chapter...of your career.

Your brand will take shape and will continue to grow and be developed over the course of your career. The concepts in *Brand You* will serve you throughout your career and throughout your life. Whether you are looking for a new job or competing for a promotion, the concept of building and communicating a unique and relevant brand never changes.

Before you go out into the real world, here is some advice that can guide you throughout your career:

Do what you love; love what you do. Always look for the job you love...the one that is so compelling that it doesn't seem like work. If you have a choice between a job that pays more and a job you love, give extra consideration to the job you love. You will be able to ultimately achieve more because you will be doing something you enjoy and competing on your strengths.

Play with passion. When you accept a job, give it 110 percent. Life is not a spectator sport. You know and other people know when you are playing with passion and when you are just playing to play. When you play with passion, you win.

Inspire people to inspire people. Your personal brand is a powerful influence on people. As you begin your career, your energy, enthusiasm, and intellectual curiosity can inspire and invigorate people with whom you work. As you gain more experience, you can be the one who supports and guides new college graduates. Wherever you are in your career, make the effort to inspire the people around you.

This semester may be over, but the concepts covered in *Brand You* will continue to serve you. Don't get discouraged if you initially don't get the phone call you want. Go back through **The 5 Steps to Real Success** and redo the key activities. Make adjustments to your cover letter, resumé, professional Web site, networking list, target company list, and your communication plan. Use the campus career center, alumni association, and library as resources and keep going. Your job is out there.

Keep *Brand You* handy and revisit **The 5 Steps to Real Success** regularly. You'll be surprised at how helpful it will be as you go through the steps when you search for your internship, your first full-time job, and even when you are making a job change.

Enjoy creating and developing your brand. The world is waiting for Brand YOU!